CASH FLOW TODAY, WEALTH TOMORROW:

The Investor's Guide to Creating Cash Flow and Equity from a Single Property

---

Henry Omelchenko

Henry Omelchenko didn't start out as a seasoned investor—he started like many people do, with a single-family home and the hope that it would slowly gain value over time. But one property taught him a powerful lesson: homes don't just sit and appreciate; they can work harder. By rethinking the way space was used, Henry turned an ordinary house into a property that produced multiple rental incomes while still holding its appeal as a single-family home.

That small experiment grew into a repeatable strategy. Over the years, Henry has applied his Single-to-Multi Conversion Strategy to transform houses into income-generating investments that deliver cash flow today and appreciation tomorrow. His approach isn't theory—it's built from hands-on projects, trial and error, and the kind of practical adjustments any investor or homeowner can follow.

Today, Henry shares what he's learned so others can unlock the hidden potential in the homes they already own—or the ones they're about to buy. His goal is straightforward: to give everyday people a roadmap to financial freedom through smarter, more flexible real estate investing.

Curated Legacy Press - USA

CASH FLOW TODAY, WEALTH TOMORROW:

The Investor's Guide to Creating Cash Flow and Equity from a Single Property

---

Introduction

Picture this: You buy a single-family home in a promising neighborhood. At first glance, it looks like a typical long-term hold play—modest rental income, steady appreciation over time, and the hope of selling at a profit years down the road.

But what if that same home could start producing *multiple streams of cash flow* immediately—without sacrificing its resale potential as a traditional single-family residence?

That's the hidden opportunity this book is about.

For decades, real estate investing has been framed through two conventional lenses:

1. **Location and timing** — when and where to buy.
2. **ROI trade-offs** — choosing between steady cash flow (usually through multifamily properties) or long-term appreciation (usually through single-family homes).

According to conventional wisdom, you can't maximize both. But that belief is a myth—and it's costing investors enormous opportunity.

This book introduces a powerful and underutilized strategy I call the **Single-to-Multi Conversion Strategy**. The concept is simple but transformative: take an ordinary single-family residence (SFR) and legally, safely, and strategically convert it into a *multi-resident rental property*. Done right, this hybrid approach allows you to:

- **Unlock immediate cash flow** by serving multiple tenants under one roof.
- **Preserve resale value** because the property can be easily reverted to its single-family form.
- **Create flexibility** in your portfolio that few other strategies can match.

In short, it's about turning today's SFR into tomorrow's high-performing asset—cash flow now, appreciation later.

Inside these pages, you'll learn how to:

- Spot properties with hidden potential for conversion.
- Navigate zoning, structural, and financing considerations with confidence.
- Design conversions that attract tenants today but can revert back for resale tomorrow.
- Apply actionable strategies, real-world case studies, and step-by-step checklists to maximize ROI.

Whether you're just starting out or scaling your portfolio, the Single-to-Multi Conversion Strategy offers a unique pathway to building wealth in real estate: **cash flow in the present, equity growth for the future**.

The chapters ahead will walk you through each step of this process—from property selection to tenant management, to exit strategy and resale—equipping you with a blueprint to invest smarter, more profitably, and with more confidence.

Henry Omelchenko

What This Book Will Outline

Part I: Foundations of Strategic Real Estate Investing

1. **Introduction to ROI in Real Estate**
    - The myths of "location, location, location" vs. structural opportunity
    - Why cash flow and appreciation need to work together
    - Introducing the "Single-to-Multi Conversion" method
2. **The Concept of Multi-Person Residences**
    - Definition: From Single-Family Residence (SFR) to Multi-Resident Rental
    - Distinguishing from traditional duplexes/triplexes
    - Case studies of successful conversions

Part II: Evaluating the Property for Conversion

3. **Structural Assessment**
    - Reading floor plans with an investor's eye
    - Identifying split potential: basements, garages, ADUs, detached units, wings
    - Utilities, plumbing, HVAC, and electrical considerations

4. **Legal and Zoning Compliance**
    - Understanding zoning codes, permits, and city variances
    - Navigating homeowner association (HOA) restrictions
    - Safety, fire codes, and rental occupancy limits

5. **Financial Feasibility**
    - Cost breakdown: construction, permits, utilities, furnishings
    - ROI calculators for multi-resident conversions
    - Financing strategies: cash, HELOCs, and private lending

---

Part III: Executing the Conversion

6. **Designing for Multiple Residents**
    - Privacy solutions: soundproofing, entrances, bathrooms
    - Creating rentable spaces without overbuilding
    - Furnished vs. unfurnished strategies
7. **Construction and Renovation Process**
    - Working with contractors and architects
    - Cost-control and timeline management
    - Pitfalls to avoid
8. **Systems for Success**
    - Parking and access solutions
    - Utilities and metering strategies
    - Technology integration: Wi-Fi, smart locks, security

Part IV: Maximizing Rental Income

9. **Tenant Targeting**
   - Ideal tenants: students, traveling nurses, seasonal workers, digital nomads
   - Lease strategies: by room vs. by floor/unit
   - Screening processes for safety and stability
10. **Property Management Models**
    - Self-management vs. property manager
    - Rental platforms (Airbnb, Zillow, Furnished Finder)
    - Conflict resolution between tenants

11. **Cash Flow Optimization**
    - Furnishing upgrades that raise rent
    - Utility chargebacks and service fees
    - Tax deductions and cost-segregation

Part V: Exit Strategy & Long-Term ROI

12. **Reversibility Back to SFR**
    - Planning the conversion with future resale in mind
    - Restoring walls, utilities, and original layouts
    - Why SFR resale value outpaces multi-unit value

13. **Market Timing and Resale Strategy**
    - When to hold vs. when to sell
    - Marketing as a turnkey SFR vs. investor-ready rental
    - Positioning for maximum buyer appeal
14. **Wealth-Building Through Repeatability**
    - Scaling the model across multiple properties
    - Creating generational wealth through hybrid investing
    - Building your personal “conversion portfolio”

PART I: Foundations of Strategic Real Estate Investing

🕮 Chapter 1: Introduction to ROI in Real Estate

Chapter 1 discusses why ROI is about more than location, compares traditional models, introduces the single-to-multi conversion strategy, and illustrates the strategy with examples and checklists.

Story Opener — *Two Doors, One Plan*

Maya and Luis stood on the sidewalk in La Quinta, palms rustling overhead, staring at a beige 4-bed/2-bath ranch with a wide side yard and a tired front door. Zillow said the neighborhood was “hot.” Their agent said it was “can’t-miss.” Their calculator said otherwise.

“If we rent it as a single,” Luis murmured, scrolling. “Market comp is about **$3,200/mo**. PITI is **$2,940**. After maintenance and a reserve? We’re barely breaking even.”

Maya didn't blink. "ROI isn't location," she said, running her fingers along the gate that separated the driveway from the backyard. "ROI is what we *do* with the location."

They walked the perimeter like detectives. The side gate opened to a concrete path that ran straight to a slider off the family room. A bonus room sat just beyond an arched opening. In the garage, a subpanel had space; the laundry room backed to a hall bath. The house wasn't screaming "flip." It was whispering "*multi*."

That night they sketched at the kitchen island:

- The oversized family room would become **two well-proportioned bedrooms** using a non-load-bearing partition with added insulation.
- The side slider would serve as a **secondary entrance** for three of the bedrooms via the side gate, preserving curb appeal.
- No kitchens in bedrooms—just a refreshed **shared kitchen**, dual fridges, and labeled pantry lockers.
- **Smart locks** on each bedroom, a mesh Wi-Fi system, and motion lighting at the gate.

Budget: **$24,500**. Timeline: **6 weeks**. The electrician recommended a **200-amp main** to comfortably handle extra fridges and window units during peak days. They permitted the partition and minor electrical; everything else was cosmetic. Crucially, they kept a folder labeled **"Reversal Plan"**—original floor plan, contractor notes, and a line-item estimate to remove the partition, patch the floors, and restore the family room when it was time to sell.

By Labor Day, the house had become a calm, well-lit hive. They listed **five rooms**:

- Four standard rooms at **$925–$975**,
- One larger corner room with a walk-in at **$1,100**.

Within two weeks, they'd placed a traveling ultrasound tech, a grad student, a solar-sales rep, and a pair of hospitality workers on staggered leases. Gross rent stabilized at **~$5,700/mo**. Expenses rose—utilities averaged **$600**, internet **$80**, cleaning of common areas **$120**—but the net cash flow jumped from near-zero to **~$1,400/mo** after a 5% vacancy reserve. The house that didn't pencil as a single suddenly performed like a small asset.

But the real trick wasn't the extra rent. It was the **way** they built it.

When the city announced a new employer moving into the valley two summers later, buyer demand swelled. Their agent called with comps: investor-style homes—locked bedroom doors, awkward exterior modifications—were selling to a narrow pool at **$535k**. Clean SFRs with open family rooms were fetching **$560–$575k**.

Maya opened the "Reversal Plan" folder. Over a single weekend, their contractor:

- Removed the partition wall and hauled it off,
- Patched and blended luxury-vinyl planks kept from the original install,
- Swapped privacy levers for standard doorknobs,
- Touched up paint and filled the gate post holes.

Cost: $7,800. The house breathed again—one large family room, a bright kitchen, and a side yard gate that looked like it had always been just a gate. They staged it lightly, leaned hard into "move-in ready SFR," and accepted an offer at **$568,000**—about **$30k** higher than the investor-only comps.

At closing, Luis flipped back through his notes:

- **24 months of net cash flow ≈ $33,000–$34,000**,
- **Equity gain** from market appreciation plus a cleaner SFR exit,
- **Minimal reversal cost** because they'd planned for it day one.

Maya smiled. "Location helped," she said, "but *design plus reversibility* made the deal."

They drove past the house a week later. A minivan was parked in the driveway; a kid's scooter leaned against the porch. The place looked exactly like what it had always been—**a single-family home**—except to the two people who knew it had quietly been a **cash-flow engine**.

Field Notes from Maya & Luis's Case

- ✅ **ROI goes beyond location.** Even in a hot neighborhood, cash flow is engineered.
- ✅ **Hybrid strategy beats either/or.** By renting by-the-room *and* preserving SFR appeal, they captured income and appreciation.
- ✅ **Reversibility is the secret sauce.** Non-structural partitions, shared-kitchen design, and a documented reversal plan protected resale.

- ✅ **Track the numbers.** Gross rent **$5,700/mo**, net cash flow **$1,400+/mo**, reversal cost **$7,800**, resale premium **$25–$35k** above investor comps.

Bridge to Chapter 1

- **Lesson 1: ROI is engineered, not inherited.** The same house produced two very different results depending on design.
- **Lesson 2: Think in systems, not just markets.** Property design, tenant mix, and reversibility all drive ROI.
- **Lesson 3: Cash flow today + equity tomorrow = investor freedom.**

Why ROI Is More Than Just Location

"Location, location, location" has been the mantra of real estate for decades. While location undoubtedly matters, many investors learn too late that a good location doesn't guarantee good cash flow. A house in a prime neighborhood can still bleed money every month if its income potential doesn't align with its expenses.

Return on Investment (ROI) is the true measure of success. It's not about the prettiest kitchen or the best zip code—it's about how effectively a property generates income while building long-term equity.

This book introduces a model that shifts the equation: **the Single-to-Multi Conversion Strategy**. By carefully transforming a single-family residence (SFR) into a multi-resident rental, investors can multiply income streams while preserving the property's long-term resale value.

Traditional ROI Models vs. The Conversion Strategy

Most investors chase ROI through:

- Buying distressed properties and flipping them.
- Holding rental SFRs for appreciation.
- Buying multi-family units (duplexes, triplexes, apartments).

Each of these has merit, but each also carries limitations:

- **Flips**: One-time profits, high risk if the market turns.
- **SFR Rentals**: Limited by a single rent check, making ROI vulnerable to vacancies.
- **Multi-Family Properties**: Higher cash flow, but resale market is limited to other investors—not to families (the largest buyer pool).

The single to multi methos overcomes these limitations by **hybridizing the best of both worlds**: steady multi-tenant cash flow *and* a broad resale market when returned to SFR form.

How ROI Expands Through Conversion

Consider a 4-bedroom home in La Quinta, California:

- As a standard SFR rental, it commands **$3,200/month**.
- After conversion into a 6-tenant multi-resident home, with each tenant paying **$950/month**, it generates **$5,700/month**.
- Expenses rise slightly (utilities, maintenance), but net cash flow nearly **doubles**.

Later, when you sell, you restore it to SFR status, attracting traditional buyers who will pay full market value. The property becomes a **cash-flow machine today and an equity play tomorrow**.

The Investor's Mindset Shift

To succeed with this model, investors must think beyond "buy and hold" and instead ask:

- How can this structure be optimized for cash flow?
- How can modifications remain reversible to protect resale?
- How do I balance tenant satisfaction with long-term equity growth?

The chapters that follow provide a step-by-step roadmap to answering these questions and applying them in the real world.

🕮 Chapter 2: The Concept of Multi-Person Residences

Chapter 2 defines the single-to-multi conversion strategy, compares it to traditional multi-family investor strategies, identifies target renters, includes a case study and checklist.

Story Opener — *The Palm Desert Experiment*

When Aisha inherited her parents' five-bedroom home in Palm Desert, she thought she had two choices: rent it out as a single lease or sell it. The neighborhood was family-friendly, the schools were good, and long-term tenants would pay about **$3,500/month**.

Her cousin, a nurse, challenged her thinking. “Why settle for one rent check,” he asked, “when you could have five or six?”

Skeptical, Aisha toured the house with a contractor. The floor plan whispered possibilities:

- The garage had its own side door and could become a **self-contained studio** without disturbing the rest of the home.
- Each of the bedrooms was large enough to command **$1,000/month** with some minor upgrades—new locks, fresh paint, and better lighting.
- Shared areas like the kitchen and living room were already oversized and could serve multiple tenants comfortably.

She invested **$18,000** in a cosmetic overhaul: durable flooring, fresh paint, and an efficient ductless mini-split in the garage. Importantly, she kept a **Reversal File** with the original floor plan, photos, and a line-item estimate to reconvert the garage and remove privacy partitions.

By spring, her tenant mix reflected exactly the sweet spot of multi-person demand:

- Two traveling nurses on six-month contracts with the local hospital.
- A graduate student from Cal State Palm Desert.
- A retired snowbird couple leasing the garage studio for the season.
- A digital nomad who paid extra for the largest corner bedroom with a walk-in closet.

Her monthly gross was now **$6,200**. Even after factoring higher utilities, Wi-Fi, and periodic cleaning of the shared kitchen, Aisha cleared nearly **$2,000 more per month** than a single lease would have produced.

Two years later, when her own family needed cash for a new business venture, she listed the house. Rather than advertise it as an "investor property," she used her Reversal File: the garage was staged as a family bonus room, the doors were reset with standard hardware, and the common areas looked like a normal home again. Within three weeks, a family with three kids purchased it for **top-of-market value**, never knowing the home had been a multi-resident cash-flow generator.

Field Notes from Aisha's Case

- ✅ **Can the property attract a diverse tenant pool?** — Nurses, students, snowbirds, and remote workers each filled a need.
- ✅ **Will conversions add cash flow without reducing comfort?** — Oversized shared spaces supported multiple residents.
- ✅ **Are modifications reversible for future resale?** — The Reversal File preserved her exit strategy.
- ✅ **Does the local market have demand for room or suite rentals?** — Proximity to hospitals, a state campus, and seasonal demand ensured strong leasing.

Bridge to Chapter 2

- **Multi-person ≠ multi-family.** Aisha's house never lost its identity as a single-family residence.
- **Tenant mix is the secret.** Diverse niches reduced vacancy risk.
- **Reversibility kept resale intact.** She exited at family-buyer prices, not discounted investor pricing.

From Single to Multi: A Subtle but Powerful Shift

The word "multi-family" often evokes apartment buildings, duplexes, or triplexes. But the **multi-person residence model** is distinct: it creates multiple rental opportunities *within* a single-family home, while maintaining its overall identity as an SFR.

It's not about transforming the house into a legally separate triplex with new addresses. It's about **strategically carving rentable spaces**—bedrooms, converted garages, basement suites—while retaining the home's resale flexibility.

How Multi-Person Residences Differ from Traditional Multi-Family

Feature	Multi-Family Property	Multi-Person SFR Conversion
Buyer Pool	Investors only	Families + investors
Cash Flow	Moderate to high	Moderate to high
Resale Value	Investor-driven (lower ceiling)	Market-driven (higher ceiling)
Flexibility	Permanent	Reversible

This distinction is critical. While traditional multi-family homes sell at a discount to SFRs on a price-per-sq-ft basis, your converted SFR retains its full resale market value.

The Sweet Spot: Who Rents These Properties?

Multi-person residences serve unique, often underserved rental markets:

- **Students** – College towns thrive on by-the-room rentals.
- **Traveling Nurses & Professionals** – Short-term room rentals near hospitals and corporate centers.
- **Seasonal Workers & Digital Nomads** – Desert communities, ski towns, and tech hubs see seasonal demand.
- **Multi-Generational Families** – Parents, children, and extended family sharing one property but desiring privacy.

By diversifying tenants, you reduce vacancy risk while increasing rental flexibility.

Case Study: The Desert Duplex Effect

A 5-bedroom SFR in Palm Desert rented for $3,500/month as a single lease. After conversion:

- Each bedroom rented individually for $1,000.
- The garage was converted into a studio that rented for $1,200.
- Gross monthly rent: $6,200.

Yet when it came time to sell, the owner marketed it as a **family home with bonus space**—and sold for top of market.

Investor Insight

The multi-person model isn't about squeezing tenants into every corner. It's about **creating functional, private, and safe living arrangements** that feel natural. When done right, tenants are happier, investors earn more, and resale value remains protected.

Investor's Checklist for Multi-Person Residences

- Can the property attract a diverse tenant pool?
- Will conversions add cash flow without reducing comfort?
- Are modifications reversible for future resale?
- Does the local market have demand for room or suite rentals?

PART II: Evaluating the Property for Conversion

📖 Chapter 3: Structural Assessment

Chapter 3 provides a detailed analysis of floor plans, infrastructure, privacy, code compliance, and reversibility, and concludes with case studies and investor checklists.

Story Opener — *The Riverside Reframe*

When Daniel first toured the 2,100 sq. ft. house in Riverside, it felt like every other four-bedroom suburban home. Beige carpet, dated fixtures, and an open-concept living room that stretched too wide for its own good. His agent saw a "starter family home." Daniel saw a blank canvas.

He unfolded the floor plan on the hood of his car and began to think like an investor, not a buyer:

- The **master suite** was enormous, large enough to be **split into two comfortable bedrooms** with a simple non-load-bearing wall.
- The **garage**, with its side entry, could be converted into a private studio with a bathroom extension.
- The oversized living room could remain communal, offering the kind of common space that makes a multi-resident home feel intentional rather than crowded.

Daniel ran the numbers: as a standard four-bedroom rental, the house could bring in about **$3,400/month**. But if reconfigured into six bedrooms plus a studio, projected rent climbed closer to **$5,600/month**.

He didn't rush. First, he ordered a **systems stress test** from his contractor. For $750, the team checked the electrical load (the 125-amp panel wasn't enough; he budgeted for a 200-amp upgrade), tested the plumbing for flow, and inspected the HVAC system. Without those checks, six extra tenants could have turned into six extra headaches.

Privacy and comfort were Daniel's next concern. He added insulation to the partition wall, upgraded interior doors, and doubled drywall between the new bedrooms. In the garage studio, he installed a ductless mini-split for independent climate control. Bathrooms were carefully balanced: four total, serving a maximum of eight tenants — right on the golden ratio of one bath per two people.

Daniel's mantra was always: *build forward, but think backward.* Every wall was designed to be removed in a weekend, every alteration logged in a binder with photos, receipts, and a budget for reversal. He wasn't just creating a cash-flowing multi-resident rental; he was protecting the home's resale identity as a single-family residence.

Within months, tenants moved in: a pair of students from UC Riverside, a traveling nurse, a young professional in tech sales, and a retired couple who leased the garage studio. The property generated **65% more income** than a standard SFR rental, and when Daniel eventually exited, the reversal plan meant a family buyer could once again see it as a simple four-bedroom home.

Field Notes from Daniel's Case

- ✅ **Floor plan adaptability:** Split master suite + garage conversion = 65% higher rent potential.
- ✅ **Infrastructure check:** Stress test revealed the need for a 200-amp panel — solved before move-in.
- ✅ **Privacy & comfort:** Insulation, soundproofing, and balanced bathrooms made the layout livable.
- ✅ **Safety & compliance:** Egress windows, detectors, and bathroom ratios met code.
- ✅ **Reversibility preserved:** All changes were temporary, logged, and costed for future removal.

Bridge to Chapter 3

- **Lesson 1: See beyond "livability."** Structural assessment is about how *many* people can live comfortably, safely, and legally — not just whether you would.
- **Lesson 2: Systems dictate success.** Electrical, plumbing, and HVAC must be stress-tested early.
- **Lesson 3: Reversible design is non-negotiable.** Plan every wall and fixture with your eventual exit in mind.

Seeing the Hidden Potential in a House

Most buyers walk through a home with one perspective: "Could I live here?"
An investor who uses the single-to-multi strategy must ask a different question:
"How many people could live here — comfortably, safely, and legally — without compromising future resale value?"

Structural assessment is the foundation of this strategy. Before permits, financing, or tenant screening come into play, you must evaluate whether the physical layout of a single-family residence can be adapted for multiple residents.

Step 1: Analyze the Floor Plan with an Investor's Eye

- **Bedrooms and Bathrooms**: Are there enough existing rooms to create private spaces? Could oversized bedrooms be divided into two functional rooms with minimal construction?
- **Living Areas**: Large living rooms, bonus rooms, and lofts can be reimagined as rentable units or common lounges.
- **Garages and Basements**: Garages can be converted into living spaces, while basements can become independent suites (where local codes allow).

Investor Example: A 2,100 sq. ft. 4-bedroom home in Riverside, California was reconfigured into a 6-bedroom rental by dividing the master suite and converting the garage. The result: rental income increased by 65%, while the home's resale profile as a SFR remained intact with reversible design choices

Step 2: Check Infrastructure for Multi-Resident Loads

1. **Electrical Capacity** – Can the panel handle multiple refrigerators, microwaves, or air conditioning units? Many SFRs run on 100-150 amps; a multi-resident conversion may require a 200-amp service.
2. **Plumbing** – Older homes often have bottleneck pipes. Adding additional bathrooms or kitchens can strain water flow and drainage unless upgraded.
3. **HVAC** – Shared systems work for SFRs, but for multiple tenants, zoning and independent climate control become critical.

Pro Tip: Hire a contractor for a "systems stress test" before purchasing. The $500–$800 spent on an inspection could save tens of thousands in retrofit surprises.

Step 3: Privacy and Accessibility

- **Entrances**: Look for ways to create separate entrances (side doors, patio sliders, breezeways) without altering the home's curb appeal.
- **Soundproofing**: Thin interior walls may need double drywall or insulation upgrades to reduce noise transfer between tenants.
- **Bathrooms**: The golden ratio in multi-tenant rentals is 1 bathroom per 2 tenants. Any less creates friction and lower rent appeal.

Step 4: Safety and Code Compliance

Before spending money, confirm:

- **Ceiling Height**: Many municipalities require at least 7 feet for habitable rooms.
- **Egress Windows**: Bedrooms must have proper escape windows in case of fire.
- **Smoke/Carbon Monoxide Detectors**: Each bedroom and hallway must meet code.

Case Study: A Phoenix investor planned to rent a converted basement as a suite, but city code required an egress window. The retrofit cost was $6,000 — wiping out six months of projected profits. Lesson: compliance always comes first.

Step 5: Future Reversibility

Your structural modifications must be **temporary or easily reversible**. That means:

- Using non-load-bearing partition walls that can be removed in a weekend.
- Avoiding permanent kitchen installations in bedrooms (a red flag for future SFR buyers).
- Keeping original floor plan drawings for resale marketing.

Think of yourself as **borrowing the house for income** — but always planning to return it to its single-family charm.

Investor's Checklist for Structural Assessment

- Does the floor plan allow for room divisions or conversions?
- Are electrical, plumbing, and HVAC sufficient for multiple tenants?
- Can separate entrances be created without harming resale appeal?
- Are bathrooms adequate for the intended tenant count?
- Do safety and zoning codes support the planned layout?
- Are all modifications reversible within a modest budget?

📖 Chapter 4: Legal and Zoning Compliance

Chapter 4 covers zoning categories, occupancy limits, HOA rules, permits, safety codes, and concludes with case examples and checklists.

Story Opener — *The Austin Surprise*

When Rachel bought a four-bedroom home near the University of Texas in Austin, she thought she'd struck gold. Her plan was simple: rent each room to students, then convert the oversized dining area into a fifth bedroom. At $850 per student, she projected **$4,250/month** in gross rent—nearly double the mortgage.

For the first semester, everything worked perfectly. Five students moved in, the rent checks came on time, and her spreadsheets looked beautiful. But in spring, she received a letter from the city: **violation of occupancy limits.**

Austin had recently cracked down on "stealth dorms," capping unrelated occupants in single-family zoned homes at **four to six maximum, depending on square footage**. Rachel's fifth tenant had pushed her over the line. She was ordered to remove one lease immediately or face fines of **$1,000/day**.

The fallout was painful. Rachel had to let one tenant go mid-semester, refund prepaid rent, and eat the vacancy. Her net income dropped, and worse, she had to disclose the violation when she later sold the property. Investors still bought it, but at a discount—she lost **$25,000** off her expected sale price.

That experience taught her what every investor learns sooner or later: you can't outsmart zoning, occupancy limits, or HOA restrictions. But you can plan for them.

Had Rachel checked Austin's revised zoning and occupancy rules before closing, she would have realized the cap and structured her leases accordingly. She might have charged slightly more per room, or targeted graduate students willing to share larger rooms, staying compliant while still improving ROI.

Field Notes from Rachel's Case

- ✅ **Zoning is the foundation.** R-1 zoning = one household; "roommate rentals" often allowed, but not full multi-family.
- ✅ **Know occupancy caps.** Rachel's market had a limit of 4–6 unrelated individuals. Exceeding this triggered fines and legal trouble.
- ✅ **HOAs can be stricter than cities.** Always review CC&Rs for tenant and rental rules before purchasing.
- ✅ **Permits protect value.** Any added bathrooms, kitchens, or major electrical/HVAC work must be permitted to avoid future red flags.
- ✅ **Safety is non-negotiable.** Detectors, egress windows, and proper fire compliance are both legal and life-saving.

Bridge to Chapter 4

- **Lesson 1: Legal clarity protects ROI.** A beautiful cash-flow model collapses under noncompliance.
- **Lesson 2: The best deals are the compliant ones.** Zoning, caps, and HOA rules shape your true strategy.
- **Lesson 3: Compliance preserves resale.** Future buyers (and lenders) want legal, safe homes—violations cost you on the back end.

Why Legal Clarity Protects ROI

The most brilliant floor plan or cash flow strategy can collapse overnight if it violates local laws. Zoning codes, occupancy limits, and safety standards exist for good reason—and ignoring them can result in fines, forced evictions, or even lawsuits.

For investors, **compliance is the first line of defense**. It not only shields you from legal trouble but also protects the value of your property when it's time to resell.

Step 1: Understand Zoning Categories

Most cities divide properties into zones such as:

- **R-1 (Single Family Residential)** – Permits one household only, but may allow accessory dwelling units (ADUs).
- **R-2, R-3, etc. (Multi-Family Residential)** – Allow duplexes, triplexes, and larger complexes.
- **Mixed Use / Special Zones** – May permit flexible housing solutions.

Investor Strategy: Even if your property is zoned R-1, many municipalities allow *room rentals* or *boarder arrangements* within that designation, provided the home retains its identity as a single household.

Step 2: Check Occupancy Limits

Local governments often enforce **"maximum occupancy" rules** such as:

- Two people per legal bedroom.
- Limits on unrelated individuals sharing a home (often 4–6 in college towns).
- Minimum square footage per person.

Case Example: In Austin, TX, the "stealth dorm" issue led to new occupancy caps. Investors renting to 8 students in a 4-bedroom house were forced to reduce to 6, lowering income. Lesson: Always know the cap *before* you buy.

Step 3: HOAs and Community Restrictions

Homeowner Associations (HOAs) can be stricter than city laws. They may:

- Prohibit short-term rentals.
- Limit the number of unrelated tenants.
- Restrict exterior modifications (separate entrances, extra parking).

Pro Tip: Always request the **CC&Rs (Covenants, Conditions, and Restrictions)** and read rental provisions carefully before purchasing.

Step 4: Permits and Variances

If your conversion involves construction:

- **Permits** are usually required for adding bathrooms, kitchens, or major electrical/HVAC upgrades.
- **Variances** may be needed if you want to add structures (e.g., detached ADUs).
- **Grandfathering** may apply if the property already has nonconforming features.

Step 5: Fire and Safety Codes

Every unit or bedroom must meet basic safety:

- Smoke and CO detectors in each bedroom and hallway.
- Proper egress windows (5.7 sq. ft. minimum opening).
- Fire-rated doors or partitions in some jurisdictions.

Skipping these isn't just illegal—it puts lives at risk and exposes you to devastating liability.

Investor's Checklist for Legal Compliance

- Zoning classification allows planned use.
- Occupancy limits researched and verified.
- HOA rules reviewed for rental restrictions.
- Permits planned for any structural work.
- Fire and safety standards met in all rooms.

🕮 Chapter 5: Financial Feasibility

Chapter 5 explains rental projections, costs, ROI/payback analysis, financing strategies, and concludes with investor checklists.

Story Opener — *The Payback Puzzle*

When Carlos bought a four-bedroom house in Riverside, his banker congratulated him. "Solid buy-and-hold," the banker said. "Rent it for $3,200 a month, cover your mortgage, and wait for appreciation."

But Carlos wasn't interested in waiting. He wanted cash flow now.

On paper, the house worked as a single rental. But when Carlos sat at his kitchen table with a spreadsheet, he started testing scenarios:

- **Scenario 1:** Rent as a single lease → $3,200/month.
- **Scenario 2:** Rent five bedrooms individually at $950 each → $4,750/month.
- **Scenario 3:** Convert the garage into a self-contained suite at $1,100/month → $5,850/month total.

That $2,650 jump in gross potential rent caught his eye.

Of course, income was only half the story. He listed every cost:

- $22,000 for garage conversion and permits.
- $12,000 for partitions, soundproofing, and upgraded locks.
- $6,000 for furnishings—basic beds, desks, and smart locks for each room.
- $2,000 in professional fees.

Total outlay: $42,000.

Now came the investor's favorite question: *When do I get my money back?*

Carlos calculated the payback period. With net cash flow increasing by about **$1,800/month** (after utilities, maintenance, and reserves), his $42,000 investment would be repaid in ~**23 months**. After that, the property would throw off pure profit.

He financed the project with a **HELOC**, drawing $45,000 at 7.25% interest. Monthly interest-only payments were about $270—easily covered by the boosted rent. From Day 1, the property cash flowed.

The secret, though, was that Carlos tracked *both sides of the coin*: the boosted income *and* the reversibility factor. Every partition was non-load-bearing. The garage had its original framing documented in a file. The furnishings were modular, designed to be removed or repurposed. When it came time to sell, he knew he could restore the home to single-family form within weeks—protecting resale value while enjoying years of extra cash flow.

Field Notes from Carlos's Case

- ✅ **Income scenarios modeled:** By-the-room and garage conversion lifted gross rent by 80% over SFR.
- ✅ **Cost clarity:** $42,000 all-in (construction, permits, furnishings, professional fees).
- ✅ **Payback period short:** ~23 months before full ROI.
- ✅ **Financing smart:** HELOC allowed cash flow from Day 1.
- ✅ **Expenses covered:** Utilities, maintenance, reserves, and management all factored in.
- ✅ **Reversibility ensured:** Every dollar spent could be undone for resale appeal.

Bridge to Chapter 5

- **Lesson 1: The numbers tell the truth.** If ROI and payback don't pencil, no vision can save the deal.
- **Lesson 2: Cash flow must be real, not theoretical.** Model utilities, maintenance, and management before committing.
- **Lesson 3: Always plan financing to support Day 1 cash flow.** Future appreciation is the bonus, not the lifeline.

The Numbers Don't Lie

A multi-resident conversion may sound promising, but investors succeed only when numbers confirm the vision. The goal is to project **income vs. expenses** with clarity—and to understand how modifications affect ROI in both the short and long term.

Step 1: Calculate Gross Potential Rent (GPR)

- **SFR Rental Model**: One lease, one payment.
- **Multi-Resident Model**: Multiple leases, multiple income streams.

Example:

- 4-bedroom SFR rents as a whole: $3,200/month.
- Same home rented by the room (5 tenants at $950 each): $4,750/month.
- Garage conversion adds a suite: +$1,100/month.
- **Total GPR: $5,850/month**.

Step 2: Estimate All-In Costs

Upfront costs vary depending on the scope of conversion:

- **Construction/Renovation**: Partition walls, soundproofing, bathroom additions.
- **Permits & Fees**: $1,500–$10,000 depending on city.
- **Furnishings**: Beds, desks, smart locks (critical for by-room rentals).
- **Professional Fees**: Architect, contractor, legal review.

Typical range: $20,000–$75,000 depending on property size and complexity.

Step 3: Model Expenses

Expenses rise slightly in multi-resident scenarios:

- **Utilities**: Higher use, though many investors pass costs to tenants.
- **Maintenance**: More wear-and-tear on shared spaces.
- **Management**: Either self-managed or 8–12% for a property manager.

- **Insurance**: Must cover higher tenant turnover and liability.

Pro Tip: Add a 10–15% contingency buffer.

Step 4: ROI and Payback Period

- **ROI Formula**: (Net Cash Flow ÷ Total Investment) × 100
- **Payback Period**: Total Investment ÷ Annual Cash Flow

Case Study:

- Total conversion cost: $40,000.
- Increased monthly cash flow: $1,800.
- Annual increase: $21,600.
- Payback Period: **1.85 years**.

After that, it's pure profit.

Step 5: Financing Options

- **Cash Reserves** – Fastest, but ties up liquidity.
- **HELOC (Home Equity Line of Credit)** – Flexible, interest-only during draw period.
- **Private Lenders** – Useful if banks shy away from unconventional use.
- **Partnerships** – Sharing risk and reward with fellow investors.

Investor Insight: Structure financing so the property cash flows from Day 1. Don't rely solely on future appreciation to bail out a poor cash-flow property.

Investor's Checklist for Financial Feasibility

- Projected rent exceeds traditional SFR rent by at least 25–40%.
- Renovation costs and payback period calculated.
- Expense increases (utilities, maintenance, insurance) accounted for.
- Financing secured with favorable terms.
- Cash reserves available for unforeseen issues.

PART III: Executing the Conversion

🕮 Chapter 6: Designing for Multiple Residents

Chapter 6 covers privacy, common areas, bathrooms, furnishings, safety enhancements, and concludes with a case study and checklists.

Story Opener — *The Phoenix Makeover*

When Jordan bought a four-bedroom ranch in Phoenix, the math looked decent but uninspiring: **$2,950/month** in rent against **$2,600** in mortgage and expenses. The spread wasn't enough to justify the headaches of landlording.

But Jordan had a vision: if the house could *comfortably* host six tenants instead of four, it could become a true income generator. The challenge? Not just squeezing in more people, but making the space livable enough to *keep* them.

He started with **privacy**. The master suite was large enough to split into two bedrooms. He insulated the new partition, added solid-core doors, and installed smart locks with unique codes.

He even included white-noise machines in each room—small details that signaled respect for tenant comfort.

Next came the **common areas**. Instead of cramming more walls into the living room, Jordan carved out a modest lounge with durable seating and high-speed Wi-Fi. The kitchen was upgraded with **two refrigerators**, labeled shelves, and wipe-clean countertops. Laundry capacity doubled with a stackable washer/dryer in the garage.

The real sticking point was **bathrooms**. With four original bedrooms, two baths had been fine. But six tenants demanded more. Jordan converted a half-bath near the garage into a full bathroom with a walk-in shower. Suddenly the ratio was three baths for six tenants—a perfect 1:2 balance.

He decided on a **hybrid furnishing model**: common spaces fully furnished for comfort and cohesion, but bedrooms left unfurnished to attract longer-term tenants who wanted to bring their own style.

The results surprised even him. Within a month, he had six tenants paying between **$950 and $1,100/month**. Turnover dropped to nearly zero because the house felt like a well-planned co-living space, not a crowded crash pad. Net cash flow nearly doubled, transforming what once looked like a break-even rental into a reliable income engine.

Field Notes from Jordan's Case

- ✅ **Privacy upgrades paid off.** Soundproofing, smart locks, and partition design raised rents by $250/room.

- ✅ **Common areas balanced.** Two fridges, labeled shelves, and a small lounge encouraged harmony.
- ✅ **Bathroom ratio optimized.** 1 bath per 2 tenants kept demand steady and complaints minimal.
- ✅ **Furnishing strategy smart.** Hybrid model attracted stable tenants while keeping turnover low.
- ✅ **Safety & comfort enhanced.** Smart locks, lighting, and storage created peace of mind.

Bridge to Chapter 6

- **Lesson 1: Design is destiny.** The way you shape the home determines rent levels, satisfaction, and turnover.
- **Lesson 2: Tenant comfort = investor profit.** Privacy, common space flow, and bathroom ratios all dictate ROI.
- **Lesson 3: Smart design protects reversibility.** Temporary partitions, modular furnishings, and well-documented upgrades keep resale value intact.

Why Design Dictates Success

Converting a single-family residence into a multi-resident rental is not just about adding walls. It's about designing a space where multiple people can live **comfortably, privately, and safely** while sharing common areas. A poorly designed layout creates tension, higher turnover, and lower rents. A smart design creates harmony—and maximizes ROI.

Step 1: Prioritize Privacy

- **Bedrooms as Mini-Sanctuaries**: Tenants will tolerate sharing kitchens and living rooms, but they demand private, quiet bedrooms.
- **Soundproofing**: Add insulation or double drywall between new partitions. White-noise machines or central HVAC fans help reduce sound transfer.
- **Separate Entrances**: Where possible, provide private access to suites or converted garages/basements.

Investor Example: A Los Angeles investor rented rooms at $850 each. After adding soundproofing and privacy locks, he raised rents to $1,100 per room with virtually no turnover.

Step 2: Balance Common Areas

- **Kitchen Flow**: Consider two refrigerators or a commercial fridge. Install durable countertops and cabinets.
- **Laundry Access**: One washer/dryer per 4–6 tenants is a comfortable ratio.
- **Living Rooms**: Don't over-shrink them. A small, shared lounge keeps tenants social and reduces isolation.

Step 3: Bathrooms – The Bottleneck Issue

Bathrooms make or break tenant satisfaction.

- **Golden Ratio**: 1 bathroom for every 2 tenants.

- **Conversions**: Half-baths can often be upgraded to full baths for modest cost.
- **Design Tip**: Pocket doors and sliding barn doors save space in tight layouts.

Step 4: Furnished vs. Unfurnished

- **Furnished Rooms**: Attract students, traveling nurses, and short-term tenants. Higher rent, faster turnover.
- **Unfurnished Rooms**: Attract long-term tenants. Lower rent, lower turnover.
- **Hybrid Model**: Some investors furnish common spaces (sofas, tables, Wi-Fi) but leave bedrooms unfurnished.

Step 5: Safety and Comfort Enhancements

- Install **smart locks** with individual codes for each tenant.
- Provide **ample lighting** inside and out—safety equals peace of mind.
- Add **storage solutions**: closets, cabinets, or even lockable cubbies.

Case Study: The Six-Bed Solution

In Phoenix, a 4-bedroom, 2-bath SFR was converted into a 6-bedroom, 3-bath residence. The investor created two additional bedrooms by reconfiguring oversized living areas. Bathrooms were upgraded with efficient fixtures. Privacy locks, a shared kitchen with dual fridges, and a small lounge completed the design. The result: 6 happy tenants, zero vacancies, and cash flow nearly doubled.

Investor's Checklist for Design

- Bedrooms designed for privacy and soundproofing.
- Kitchens and laundry sized for tenant count.
- Bathrooms upgraded to meet 1:2 tenant ratio.
- Furnished/unfurnished strategy aligned with target market.
- Safety measures (smart locks, lighting, storage) included.

🕮 Chapter 7: Construction and Renovation Process

Chapter 7 covers assembling a team, managing timelines, cost control, pitfalls, documentation, and concludes with a checklist.

Story Opener — *The Sacramento Sprint*

When Priya closed on a three-bedroom ranch in Sacramento, her plan was tight: convert it into a five-bedroom rental in under ten weeks, keep costs under $45,000, and have tenants lined up before the fall semester began.

She knew the danger of this phase: design was just paper until someone picked up a hammer. Execution could make or break her ROI.

Step 1: Assembling the team. Priya didn't go with the cheapest contractor she found on Craigslist. Instead, she interviewed three, specifically asking: *"Have you worked with investors doing rooming conversions, not just flips?"* Only one could answer with actual references from other multi-resident investors. She hired him and added a permit runner who specialized in expediting approvals with Sacramento's notoriously slow planning office.

Step 2: Timeline management. The project was broken into phases:

- **Weeks 1–2:** Demo and prep—removing non-load-bearing walls, roughing in plumbing.
- **Weeks 3–7:** Build phase—new partitions, upgraded bathrooms, added soundproofing.
- **Weeks 8–9:** Finishes—painting, flooring, trim.
- **Week 10:** Furnishing—locks, appliances, Wi-Fi.

Priya checked progress twice a week. When a supplier delayed flooring, she approved a mid-grade alternative on the spot, saving two weeks of downtime.

Step 3: Cost control. She handled painting and furniture assembly herself, saving about **$12,000**. She left electrical and plumbing strictly to licensed pros, avoiding dangerous DIY mistakes. Mid-grade materials—durable but not luxury—kept her on budget while standing up to tenant wear and tear.

Step 4: Avoiding pitfalls. Her contractor pushed for recessed lighting throughout. "It'll make the place shine," he said. Priya pulled out her plan. "Not in the budget, not in the ROI." Scope creep denied.

Step 5: Documentation. Every receipt went into a shared Google Drive. She snapped before-and-after photos for marketing and logged warranties for appliances. By the time tenants toured, she already had a photo package that made the listing look like a boutique co-living space.

The result: a **five-bedroom, three-bath** multi-resident rental completed in just under nine weeks. Priya hit her budget, had tenants lined up, and—because of her documentation—was positioned for both smooth tax deductions and a future resale exit.

Field Notes from Priya's Case

- ✅ **Team choice matters.** Contractors with investor experience avoid rookie mistakes.
- ✅ **Timeline phases enforced.** Demo, build, finishes, furnishing—kept her on track.
- ✅ **Costs balanced.** Mid-grade durable finishes + DIY painting/furniture saved $12,000.
- ✅ **Scope creep resisted.** Stuck to ROI-focused plan, not flashy add-ons.
- ✅ **Documentation doubled as marketing.** Photos, receipts, and warranties added value for tenants, taxes, and resale.

Bridge to Chapter 7

- **Lesson 1: Execution is where ROI lives or dies.** Even great designs fail without disciplined construction management.
- **Lesson 2: Budgets must serve strategy.** Durable mid-grade materials protect profit margins.
- **Lesson 3: Documentation builds long-term equity.** Photos, receipts, and warranties pay off for both tenants and resale buyers.

Turning Design Into Reality

Once you've finalized your plan, the next step is execution. This phase transforms vision into rentable space—and it's where budgets and timelines often spiral out of control if not managed carefully.

Step 1: Assemble the Right Team

- **Contractor**: Choose someone familiar with small-scale conversions, not just cosmetic flips.
- **Architect/Designer**: For major reconfigurations (e.g., garage or basement conversions).
- **Permit Specialist**: In some cities, hiring a permit runner speeds up approvals.
- **Handyman/Trades**: Reliable electricians, plumbers, HVAC technicians.

Pro Tip: Interview multiple contractors. Ask for references specifically from rental investors—not just homeowners.

Step 2: Manage the Timeline

- **Phase 1 – Demo & Prep**: Remove walls, prep plumbing/electrical (1–2 weeks).
- **Phase 2 – Build**: Add partitions, install bathrooms/kitchens, soundproofing (3–6 weeks).
- **Phase 3 – Finishing**: Flooring, painting, trim work (2 weeks).
- **Phase 4 – Furnishing & Setup**: Install locks, Wi-Fi, appliances (1 week).

Typical timeline: **6–10 weeks** depending on complexity.

Step 3: Control Costs Without Cutting Corners

- **Materials**: Use durable mid-grade finishes. Cheap products wear out fast; luxury finishes don't pay back in rentals.
- **Labor**: Bundle tasks (e.g., painter also doing drywall touch-ups).
- **DIY vs. Professional**: Do painting, basic landscaping, or minor installs yourself; leave electrical, plumbing, and structural work to pros.

Case Example: A Sacramento investor saved $12,000 by doing interior painting, flooring, and furniture assembly himself, while outsourcing plumbing and electrical.

Step 4: Avoid the Pitfalls

- **Scope Creep**: Stick to the plan. Don't let contractors talk you into unnecessary "upgrades."
- **Permit Delays**: Submit paperwork early; delays can stall projects for months.
- **Tenant Readiness**: Don't rush tenants in before the property is fully safe and complete.

Step 5: Document Everything

- Keep before-and-after photos for marketing.
- Save all receipts for tax deductions and resale documentation.
- Record contractor warranties and material guarantees.

Investor's Checklist for Renovation

- Contractor and team vetted with investor references.
- Timeline mapped out and monitored weekly.
- Costs controlled with mid-grade durable materials.
- Pitfalls (scope creep, delays) anticipated.
- Documentation saved for taxes and resale.

🕮 Chapter 8: Systems for Success

Chapter 8 covers parking, utilities, internet, smart tech, shared space management, conflict systems, and concludes with a checklist.

Story Opener — *The San Diego Setup*

When Marco turned his San Diego bungalow into a six-tenant rental, the renovations went smoothly. But within weeks of move-in, the problems began:

- Tenants fought over **parking spaces** in the cramped driveway.
- The **Wi-Fi lagged** every night when everyone streamed Netflix.
- Utility bills spiked, and no one wanted to admit who ran the A/C nonstop.
- The kitchen turned into a battlefield of dirty dishes and "borrowed" food.

Marco realized design alone wasn't enough. Without **systems**, the house would unravel.

He got to work:

- **Parking:** He painted clear lines in the driveway and created a rotation system for the street spots. The simple fix ended 80% of the complaints.
- **Utilities:** Instead of splitting bills each month, he added a **flat $100 utility fee** to every lease. This not only covered his average costs but created a small monthly buffer.
- **Internet:** He invested in a **mesh Wi-Fi system** with fiber internet, eliminating coverage dead zones. The nightly "buffering wars" vanished.
- **Tech integration:** Each tenant got a unique **smart lock code**. When one tenant moved out, Marco deleted the code in seconds. He also added a **smart thermostat**, keeping cooling costs predictable.
- **Shared space management:** He hired a cleaner twice a month, folding the cost into rent. Tenants stopped arguing over chores, and the kitchen stayed functional.
- **Conflict prevention:** A one-page **house rules addendum** spelled out noise limits, guest policies, and cleaning expectations. Marco created a group chat for quick communication, and offered a $50 rent discount to a "house captain" who served as liaison.

By the end of the second lease cycle, turnover dropped dramatically. Marco's tenants felt safe, connected, and fairly treated—allowing him to justify slightly higher rents than competing room rentals nearby.

Field Notes from Marco's Case

- ✅ **Parking clarity matters.** Painted lines + clear assignments reduced disputes.
- ✅ **Utility billing simplified.** Flat $100 fee covered costs and added a small profit center.
- ✅ **High-speed internet is non-negotiable.** Mesh Wi-Fi solved tenant complaints.
- ✅ **Smart tech saves time.** Smart locks and thermostats streamlined management.
- ✅ **Shared space harmony.** Professional cleaning + house rules maintained peace.
- ✅ **Conflict prevention pays.** Group chat and a designated "house captain" improved communication.

Bridge to Chapter 8

- **Lesson 1: Systems sustain cash flow.** Renovations attract tenants, but systems keep them.
- **Lesson 2: Clarity beats conflict.** Parking, utilities, and rules eliminate gray areas.
- **Lesson 3: Smart tools protect your time.** Technology and house management systems scale with you as you grow.

Why Systems Matter

Design and construction create the physical foundation, but systems are what make a multi-resident rental run smoothly. Without proper systems, tenants clash, expenses balloon, and turnover spikes. With them, you create a seamless living experience that justifies higher rent and minimizes headaches.

Step 1: Parking and Access Solutions

- **Parking**: One of the biggest tenant complaints. If the property can't accommodate one car per resident, establish clear parking assignments (driveway vs. street).
- **Entrances**: Secondary entrances (sliding doors, side gates, breezeways) allow tenants privacy and reduce traffic through one main door.
- **Security**: Install cameras at main access points. Tenants appreciate safety, and you protect your investment.

Investor Tip: Use clearly marked parking lines or signage. This small step prevents 80% of parking disputes.

Step 2: Utilities and Billing

- **Shared Utilities**: Most conversions keep one set of utilities. Investors can either bundle utilities into rent or add a flat monthly utility fee.

- **Sub-Metering**: In some markets, it may be worth installing separate meters for water or electricity (though upfront costs can be high).
- **Internet/Wi-Fi**: Critical. Invest in high-speed fiber or mesh systems to cover large homes. Poor Wi-Fi = tenant complaints.

Case Example: An investor in San Diego included high-speed internet and a flat $100/month utility fee in each tenant's lease. The utility fee exceeded average costs, creating a modest profit center.

Step 3: Technology Integration

- **Smart Locks**: Assign unique codes to each tenant. Codes can be changed remotely at move-out.
- **Smart Thermostats**: Help control HVAC costs in large shared homes.
- **Cameras & Lighting**: Exterior only—respect tenant privacy but ensure security.

Step 4: Shared Space Management

- **Cleaning Rotations**: Tenants take turns, or you hire a cleaner (common in higher-end markets).
- **Appliance Durability**: Invest in commercial-grade washers/dryers or at least high-capacity models.
- **Furnishings**: Choose durable, stain-resistant materials for couches, chairs, and flooring.

Step 5: Conflict Prevention Systems

- **House Rules**: Written agreements about noise, guests, smoking, and cleanliness.
- **Communication Channels**: Group chats or property management apps keep everyone aligned.
- **Manager Role**: Either self-managed or designate a tenant "house captain" with a rent discount.

Investor's Checklist for Systems

- Parking plan and security measures in place.
- Utility billing strategy decided (bundled vs. flat fee).
- High-speed internet and smart technology installed.
- Shared spaces furnished with durable materials.
- House rules and conflict resolution system established.

PART IV: Maximizing Rental Income

🕮 Chapter 9: Tenant Targeting

Chapter 9 covers tenant niches, lease structures, screening, marketing channels, managing tenant mix, and concludes with a checklist.

Story Opener — *The Las Vegas Match*

When Elena bought a five-bedroom home near the Las Vegas Strip, her first thought was students. UNLV was only a few miles away, and demand for affordable housing was strong. But she hesitated—students brought high turnover, late-night parties, and frequent damage.

Instead, she tested a different niche: **traveling nurses**. With three major hospitals nearby, she listed her rooms on **Furnished Finder**. Her ad highlighted fast Wi-Fi, furnished bedrooms with desks, and quiet common spaces.

The response was immediate. Within two weeks, she had four nurses on three-to-six-month contracts, each paying **25% more** than what students typically offered. Occupancy ran above **95%**, and her tenants appreciated the stability of a home environment compared to extended-stay hotels.

For the garage suite, she targeted a different market: a professional couple working in the hospitality industry. A slightly higher rent premium kept the tenant mix balanced.

The key was **compatibility**. Elena avoided combining students with professionals, knowing lifestyle clashes could derail her property. She set quiet hours, required co-signed leases for any short-term guests, and used a hybrid lease structure—six months for professionals, three months for nurses on rotation.

Her rental income exceeded projections, but more importantly, her **turnover costs plummeted**. Instead of constant tenant churn, she had reliable, respectful renters who treated the house as a shared professional residence.

Field Notes from Elena's Case

- ✅ **Market niches defined.** Chose traveling nurses and professionals over students for stability.
- ✅ **Lease terms aligned.** Nurses signed 3–6 months; professionals 6–12 months.
- ✅ **Screening solid.** Verified employment, required co-signers where needed.
- ✅ **Marketing channels optimized.** Furnished Finder attracted high-paying professionals.
- ✅ **Tenant mix balanced.** Compatible lifestyles reduced conflict and turnover.

Bridge to Chapter 9

- **Lesson 1: The right tenants = the right ROI.** Not all renters are created equal; niches dictate returns.
- **Lesson 2: Match lease structure to tenant type.** Terms should reflect each niche's needs.
- **Lesson 3: Tenant harmony drives profitability.** A balanced, compatible tenant mix lowers turnover and maximizes cash flow.

The Right Tenants = The Right ROI

Not every property is right for every tenant, and not every tenant is right for a multi-resident home. Choosing the right **tenant demographic** is the difference between a harmonious, profitable house and a constant revolving door of problems.

Step 1: Identify Your Market Niches

1. **Students** – Reliable in college towns. Often rent by the semester. Parents usually co-sign.
2. **Traveling Nurses & Professionals** – Higher rent potential, shorter stays. Best in cities with hospitals or corporate centers.
3. **Digital Nomads** – Attracted to furnished rooms with fast internet. Seasonal stays.
4. **Seasonal/Resort Workers** – Common in ski towns, beach towns, and desert resorts.
5. **Multi-Generational Families** – Particularly strong in suburban or cultural markets.

Step 2: Lease Structures

- **By the Room**: Most common, maximizes rent.
- **By the Suite**: Garage conversions or basement apartments appeal to professionals or couples.
- **Hybrid**: Some rooms by the month, others as long-term leases.

Investor Tip: Match lease terms to tenant type. Students = semester leases. Professionals = 6–12 months. Digital nomads = 3–6 months.

Step 3: Screening for Stability

- **Credit & Background Checks**: Non-negotiable.
- **Employment Verification**: Especially for professionals.
- **Co-Signers**: Students often require parents to co-sign.
- **References**: Ask for prior landlord references.

Step 4: Marketing Channels

- **Zillow / Apartments.com** – Good for long-term tenants.
- **Furnished Finder** – Excellent for nurses and traveling professionals.
- **Airbnb / VRBO** – Short-term, but can fill gaps.
- **Craigslist / Facebook Marketplace** – Useful for local renters but requires careful screening.

Case Example: A Las Vegas investor marketed rooms on Furnished Finder to traveling nurses, charging 25% higher rents than the local student market. Occupancy remained above 95%.

Step 5: Managing Tenant Mix

- Aim for **compatible lifestyles**: mixing students and professionals often creates tension.
- Establish **quiet hours** to reduce conflicts.
- Encourage community but protect privacy.

Investor's Checklist for Tenant Targeting

- Market niches identified for property location.
- Lease structures aligned with tenant type.
- Screening procedures standardized.
- Marketing channels selected and listings optimized.
- Tenant mix strategy designed for harmony.

🕮 Chapter 10: Property Management Models

Chapter 10 discusses self, professional, hybrid management, tools, style, and concludes with an investor checklist.

Story Opener — *The San Jose House Captain*

Sofia owned a six-bedroom rental in San Jose and tried self-managing for the first six months. At first, it seemed easy: collect rent, answer the occasional maintenance call, and check in with tenants. But soon, her phone became a 24/7 hotline.

- A clogged sink at 11 p.m.
- Arguments over cleaning schedules.
- Missed rent from a tenant who "forgot" for the third time.

Sofia was burning out. Hiring a professional manager wasn't ideal—quotes came back at **10% of gross rent**, and none of the firms specialized in by-the-room rentals. She needed a middle ground.

That's when she tried the **house captain model**. She offered one responsible tenant—a software engineer—a **$150 monthly rent discount** in exchange for managing minor issues:

organizing cleaning rotations, monitoring parking disputes, and reporting maintenance problems.

The change was immediate. Sofia's weekly involvement dropped by **70%**, and issues were resolved before they escalated. She still handled leasing and rent collection, but the day-to-day friction disappeared.

She also layered in **tools for efficiency**: a group WhatsApp chat for quick communication, smart locks for easy tenant turnover, and RentRedi to automate rent collection. With systems in place, she could scale her portfolio without drowning in calls.

By staying professional—quarterly inspections, firm rules, and consistent enforcement—Sofia created a balance: tenants felt supported, the property stayed in good condition, and she kept most of her profit without burning out.

Field Notes from Sofia's Case

- ✅ **Self-management works—but only if local and organized.** Burnout risk is high.
- ✅ **Professional managers are best for scale or distance.** But many don't understand multi-resident models.
- ✅ **Hybrid model wins in-between.** House captain + partial outsourcing saved time and money.
- ✅ **Tools amplified efficiency.** Smart locks, rent software, and group chats reduced friction.
- ✅ **Management style matters.** Professional tone, clear expectations, and quarterly inspections built tenant trust.

Bridge to Chapter 10

- **Lesson 1: Management defines profitability.** Bad management wipes out good design and legal compliance.
- **Lesson 2: Choose a model that fits your stage.** Self, hybrid, or professional—each works when aligned with scale and location.
- **Lesson 3: Leverage tools and systems.** Technology and communication strategies keep multi-resident rentals running smoothly.

Why Management Defines Profitability

Even the best-designed, legally compliant, and fully rented property can fail if poorly managed. Multi-resident rentals are unique: they require more oversight than single-family rentals but less than large apartment complexes. The right management model keeps tenants happy, protects your property, and sustains profitability.

Step 1: Self-Management

- **Pros**:
  - Maximum profit (no manager fees).
  - Direct relationship with tenants.
  - Immediate control over repairs and rules.
- **Cons**:
  - Time-intensive—tenant issues can arise at any hour.
  - Emotional stress if tenants clash.
  - Requires strong organization and boundary-setting.

Best For: Investors starting out, living close to their property, and willing to learn management skills.

Step 2: Professional Property Management

- **Pros**:
  - Handles marketing, screening, rent collection, and tenant issues.
  - Enforces house rules objectively.
  - Provides access to vendor networks for repairs.
- **Cons**:
  - Fees range from 8–12% of gross rent.
  - Not all property managers understand by-the-room rentals—many are trained for traditional SFR leases.

Best For: Investors scaling portfolios or living out-of-state.

Step 3: Hybrid Management

- **House Captain Model**: Designate one responsible tenant as a "house leader" who oversees minor issues (cleaning schedules, reporting problems). Offer a rent discount as compensation.
- **Partial Outsourcing**: You manage leasing and tenant placement, but outsource maintenance or accounting.

Investor Example: A San Jose investor gave one tenant a $150/month discount to act as house captain. This reduced her management time by 70% while keeping oversight costs low.

Step 4: Tools for Efficiency

- **Property Management Software**: Buildium, AppFolio, or RentRedi streamline rent collection and maintenance requests.
- **Smart Tech**: Remote access locks and smart thermostats reduce in-person management.
- **Communication**: Group chats (WhatsApp, Slack) keep tenants aligned and reduce miscommunication.

Step 5: Management Style Matters

Clear rules + consistent enforcement = stable tenants.

- **Set Expectations Early**: House rules and lease agreements must be crystal clear.
- **Stay Professional**: Treat tenants as clients, not friends.
- **Inspect Regularly**: Quarterly walkthroughs catch issues before they become costly.

Investor's Checklist for Property Management

- Management model chosen (self, professional, hybrid).
- House rules established and enforced consistently.
- Technology tools integrated for efficiency.
- Clear communication channels in place.
- Regular inspection schedule maintained.

🕮 Chapter 11: Cash Flow Optimization

Chapter 11 discusses rent premiums, add-on revenues, expense reduction, tax strategies, scalability, and concludes with case examples and a checklist.

Story Opener — *The Denver Upgrade*

Samantha owned a six-bedroom rental in Denver that was already performing well. Her tenants were happy, occupancy was steady, and cash flow was positive. But she wondered: *Am I leaving money on the table?*

She decided to test a few strategic upgrades.

First, she invested **$9,000** to add compact en-suite bathrooms to two of the bedrooms. Overnight, those rooms went from **$950/month** to **$1,400/month**. That was an extra **$10,800 per year** from just two tenants.

Next, she reviewed add-on revenue. Parking in Denver was tight, so she began charging **$75/month** for the two reserved driveway spots. Both were taken immediately. She also added a flat **$100 utility fee** to each lease, structured slightly above average usage. With six tenants, that created a small but reliable monthly buffer.

On the expense side, Samantha replaced all common area lights with **LEDs**, installed a **smart thermostat**, and swapped in **durable vinyl plank flooring**. Maintenance calls dropped, utility bills shrank, and turnover costs decreased because flooring no longer had to be patched or replaced every year.

Finally, she met with a CPA who specialized in real estate. By applying accelerated depreciation through a **cost segregation study**, she shaved thousands off her taxable income, boosting her after-tax ROI by nearly **15%**.

The changes weren't dramatic—they didn't alter the property's character or reversibility—but together they snowballed into nearly **$20,000 in additional annual profit**. That extra cash flow went straight into savings for her next down payment.

Field Notes from Samantha's Case

- ✅ **Rent premiums captured.** En-suite upgrades boosted two rooms by $450/month each.
- ✅ **Add-on income streams added.** Parking and utility fees created consistent side revenue.
- ✅ **Expenses reduced.** LEDs, smart thermostat, and durable flooring cut costs.
- ✅ **Preventive maintenance scheduled.** Quarterly checks avoided emergencies.
- ✅ **Tax strategy leveraged.** Cost segregation and deductions raised after-tax ROI.

Bridge to Chapter 11

- **Lesson 1: Optimization compounds.** Small improvements add up to thousands per year.
- **Lesson 2: Focus on both sides of the equation.** Raise income *and* reduce expenses without sacrificing tenant satisfaction.
- **Lesson 3: Profit fuels scale.** Each optimized property accelerates portfolio growth.

The Art of Maximizing Returns

Once your property is rented and managed, the focus shifts to optimization—finding ways to increase income and reduce expenses without sacrificing tenant satisfaction. Small improvements can compound into thousands of dollars in annual profit.

Step 1: Rental Income Enhancements

- **Furnishing Premiums**: Furnished rooms can command 15–30% higher rents.
- **Shorter Leases**: Month-to-month or 3-month leases offer flexibility that some tenants will pay extra for.
- **Suite Upgrades**: Garage or basement units with private bathrooms fetch higher rents than standard rooms.

Case Example: A Denver investor upgraded two bedrooms with en-suite baths. Rent jumped from $950 to $1,400 each—a $10,800 annual increase.

Step 2: Add-On Revenue Streams

- **Utilities & Internet**: Charge flat fees slightly above average usage.
- **Parking Fees**: Reserved driveway or garage spots can generate $50–$100/month.
- **Laundry**: Coin-op or app-based washers/dryers create small but steady income.
- **Cleaning Services**: Offer optional monthly cleaning for a fee.

Step 3: Expense Reduction Strategies

- **Energy Efficiency**: LED lighting, smart thermostats, and low-flow fixtures reduce bills.
- **Durable Materials**: Mid-grade, high-durability flooring and paint reduce turnover costs.
- **Preventive Maintenance**: Quarterly inspections prevent expensive emergencies.

Step 4: Tax Optimization

- **Depreciation**: Each structural improvement adds to your depreciation schedule.
- **Cost Segregation Studies**: Accelerate depreciation of certain assets.

- **Expense Deductions**: Travel, repairs, utilities, and even furnishings are deductible.

Pro Tip: Work with a CPA familiar with real estate investing. A well-structured tax plan can increase ROI by 10–20%.

Step 5: Scaling with Profitability

The real power of optimization is scalability. Each property becomes more profitable, allowing reinvestment into new acquisitions. Over time, this snowballs into portfolio growth.

Investor's Checklist for Cash Flow Optimization

- Rent premiums applied for furnished or upgraded rooms.
- Add-on revenue streams implemented (parking, utilities, services).
- Energy efficiency upgrades completed.
- Preventive maintenance schedule enforced.
- Tax strategy reviewed with a CPA.

PART V: Exit Strategy & Long-Term ROI

📖 Chapter 12: Reversibility Back to SFR

Chapter 12 covers planning reversible modifications, documentation, budgeting, marketing flexibility, curb appeal, and concludes with an investor checklist.

Story Opener — *The Phoenix Payoff*

When Martin bought a four-bedroom ranch in Phoenix, he converted the garage into a sleek studio suite with its own bath and kitchenette. For three years, it brought in an extra **$1,200/month**, turning an average rental into a cash-flow star.

But when Martin decided to sell, his agent warned him: "If we list this as an 'investor property,' you'll shrink your buyer pool. Families don't want to see a chopped-up house. Investors will lowball you."

Fortunately, Martin had planned for this from day one. He opened his **conversion binder**—a file with original floor plans, permits, receipts, and photos of the house before and after the conversion. He had even kept a budget line for **reversibility costs**.

In two weeks, his contractor:

- Removed the kitchenette and capped the plumbing.
- Restored the garage door opener and neutral paint.
- Smoothed over partition walls in the main house.

Total cost: $9,000.

The house was once again a classic four-bedroom SFR with a clean garage, fresh paint, and family-friendly curb appeal.

Listed this way, it sold not to an investor, but to a young family relocating from California. They paid **$85,000 more** than investor comps for similar "chopped-up" houses nearby.

Martin walked away smiling: he had enjoyed **three years of extra cash flow** and then exited with **top-of-market resale value**, all because he designed with reversibility in mind.

Field Notes from Martin's Case

- ✅ **Planned for reversibility early.** Non-load-bearing partitions, capped plumbing, and neutral entrances made restoration easy.
- ✅ **Kept documentation.** Conversion binder reassured buyers and appraisers.

- ✅ **Budgeted for reversal.** $9,000 restoration cost unlocked $85,000 in resale value.
- ✅ **Marketed flexibility.** Highlighted "family home with optional income potential."
- ✅ **Preserved curb appeal.** No exterior features screamed "multi-family."

Bridge to Chapter 12

- **Lesson 1: Reversibility protects value.** Multi-resident rentals only deliver long-term ROI if they can return to SFR form.
- **Lesson 2: Documentation builds trust.** Buyers and appraisers want proof that modifications are safe and reversible.
- **Lesson 3: Flexibility expands your buyer pool.** Market to both families and investors to maximize exit options.

Why Reversibility Protects Long-Term Value

The beauty of the single-to-multi model lies in its **dual nature**: today, it's a cash-flow machine; tomorrow, it can be restored to a traditional single-family home (SFR). Since SFRs have a much larger buyer pool than multi-family properties, reversibility is the safeguard that preserves resale value and maximizes exit options.

Step 1: Plan for Reversibility from Day One

- **Temporary Walls**: Use non-load-bearing partitions that can be removed without structural changes.
- **Minimal Plumbing Additions**: Avoid adding full kitchens in bedrooms; opt for mini-fridges and microwaves instead.
- **Flexible Entrances**: Secondary entrances (like sliders or breezeway gates) should blend seamlessly into the home once converted back.

Investor Tip: Keep the original floor plan drawings in a file. Buyers love to see how the house can return to its "intended" layout.

Step 2: Document Every Modification

- Maintain a "conversion binder" with contractor receipts, permits, and before-and-after photos.
- This helps in two ways:
    1. Buyers trust documented reversibility.
    2. You may be able to claim tax deductions on improvements during the rental phase.

Step 3: Budget for Reversal

Plan early for the cost of returning the home to SFR form.

- Removing walls: $1,000–$3,000.
- Restoring garage: $5,000–$12,000.
- Repainting and refreshing: $2,000–$6,000.

Case Example: An investor in Phoenix spent $9,000 reversing a garage suite back into a standard garage. The resale price of the SFR was $85,000 higher than if marketed as an "investor-only" property.

Step 4: Highlight Flexibility in Marketing

When selling, emphasize:

- "This home can serve as a traditional single-family residence **or** an income-generating property."
- Market both to families (largest pool) and investors (smaller pool but higher ROI vision).

Step 5: Protect Curb Appeal

Exterior changes should always be **neutral and reversible**. Avoid adding visible features (extra doors, external plumbing) that scream "multi-family."

Investor's Checklist for Reversibility

- All modifications are non-structural or easily reversed.
- Documentation binder maintained for buyers and appraisers.
- Budget reserved for restoration before resale.
- Marketing plan highlights dual potential (SFR + investment).
- Curb appeal preserved as family-friendly.

📖 Chapter 13: Market Timing and Resale Strategy

Chapter 13 covers understanding market cycles, buyer pools, appraisal strategies, resale prep, exit scenarios, and concludes with an investor checklist.

Story Opener — *The Palm Desert Pivot*

For three years, Anita's Palm Desert rental printed money. Converted from a four-bedroom into a five-bedroom with a garage suite, it netted **$55,000** in cash flow during her hold period. But Anita knew cash flow was only half the story—timing the exit would determine her true wealth gain.

She kept one eye on the market. When inventory was high and sales sluggish, she held the property, content with steady rental income. But when the desert market tightened—low inventory, bidding wars, and buyers pouring in from Los Angeles—she decided it was time.

Step one was **reversibility**. She removed interior locks, restored the garage to its original use, and staged the home as a warm single-family residence. The cosmetic refresh was simple: new paint, desert-friendly landscaping, and modern light fixtures.

Her agent listed the property in two ways:

- As a **move-in ready SFR**, appealing to families.
- With a subtle note about its potential as an **income-producing property**, appealing to hybrid buyers and investors.

The appraisal came in based on **SFR comps**, not income valuation, which boosted the number. Within two weeks, Anita accepted an offer that delivered an **$120,000 equity gain**—on top of the three years of steady cash flow.

By timing her exit to coincide with a seller's market and leaning into reversibility, Anita effectively doubled her ROI.

Field Notes from Anita's Case

- ✅ **Watched market cycles.** Held during soft market, sold during strong seller's market.
- ✅ **Targeted multiple buyer pools.** Families, investors, and hybrid buyers widened demand.
- ✅ **Chose appraisal strategy wisely.** Restored SFR layout secured a higher valuation.
- ✅ **Prepped resale smartly.** Cosmetic updates + neutral staging maximized appeal.
- ✅ **Exit aligned with goals.** Combined $55,000 net cash flow + $120,000 equity gain for doubled ROI.

Bridge to Chapter 13

- **Lesson 1: Timing is leverage.** Hold when the market is soft; sell when demand surges.
- **Lesson 2: Know your buyers.** Families pay premiums, investors value cash flow, hybrids want both.
- **Lesson 3: Restoration equals reward.** Reversibility and cosmetic prep expand buyer pools and maximize appraisals.

The Power of Timing

Real estate wealth is often determined not only by what you buy, but by **when you sell**. Multi-resident conversions give you flexibility: you can hold for cash flow during slower markets and sell as a SFR when demand is strong.

Step 1: Watch Market Cycles

- **Seller's Market**: High buyer demand, low inventory. Best time to restore to SFR and sell for top dollar.
- **Buyer's Market**: High inventory, slow sales. Better to hold the property as a cash-flowing multi-resident rental.
- **Neutral Market**: Evaluate whether cash flow exceeds appreciation potential.

Step 2: Know Your Buyer Pools

- **Families**: Represent 70–80% of the market. They pay premium prices for SFRs.
- **Investors**: Smaller pool but may pay well for a proven income property.
- **Hybrid Buyers**: Increasingly, buyers want both—a home they can live in while renting out parts for income.

Step 3: Optimize Appraisals

- **SFR Appraisal**: Based on comparable single-family homes. This usually yields a higher valuation.
- **Income Appraisal**: Based on rental income. Useful when selling to investors but often lower than SFR valuation.

Investor Strategy: Restore to SFR layout to ensure a family-focused appraisal, even if marketing to investors too.

Step 4: Strategic Resale Preparation

- **Cosmetic Refresh**: Fresh paint, landscaping, updated fixtures—small costs, big ROI.
- **Neutralize Modifications**: Remove locks on every bedroom, replace partition walls with open layouts.
- **Stage Thoughtfully**: Showcase the home as a family residence while also mentioning rental flexibility in the listing description.

Step 5: Exit Scenarios

1. **Cash Flow Hold**: Delay selling until the market strengthens while enjoying monthly income.
2. **Hybrid Marketing**: List as both SFR and income property to attract multiple buyer types.
3. **Portfolio Sale**: Package multiple conversions and sell to an institutional investor.

Case Example: A Palm Desert investor held a 5-bedroom multi-resident property for 3 years, generating $55,000 net cash flow. When the market surged, he restored it to SFR form and sold for a $120,000 gain. The dual benefit doubled his overall ROI.

Investor's Checklist for Market Timing & Resale

- Current market cycle assessed (buyer vs. seller market).
- Buyer pool identified (families, investors, or hybrid).
- Appraisal strategy chosen (SFR vs. income).
- Cosmetic and layout restoration planned.
- Exit strategy aligned with cash flow and equity goals.

📖 Chapter 14: Wealth-Building Through Repeatability

Chapter 14 covers creating a repeatable system, scaling with financing, diversifying markets, building teams, transitioning from income to legacy, and concludes with a case study and investor checklist.

Story Opener — *The Riverside Portfolio*

A decade ago, David bought his first SFR in Riverside, California. It was a modest three-bedroom ranch, but with a garage conversion and a partitioned living room, it became a six-tenant rental that generated nearly **$2,000/month in net cash flow**.

That success didn't just pay the bills—it lit a path.

David created a **repeatable system**. He defined his "buy box": homes between 1,800–2,400 sq. ft., in working-class neighborhoods near colleges or hospitals, with large living areas and simple garage layouts. He built a **conversion template**: temporary partitions, 200-amp electrical upgrades, dual fridges, and smart locks. He standardized his tenant mix around traveling nurses, graduate students, and young professionals.

Each property followed the same playbook.

By year five, David owned **five conversions**, all producing steady cash flow. He used a **HELOC** on his first home to fund the second, then qualified for portfolio loans to acquire more. Partnerships helped him expand into medical hubs and suburban corridors outside his hometown.

The key wasn't improvisation—it was **scalability**. Every property was documented, every contractor knew the plan, and every manager had clear systems to follow.

By year ten, David had converted **eight homes**. He sold half during a seller's market, restoring them to SFRs and capturing top-dollar resale value. The others he held for ongoing income. In total, he cleared over **$2 million** in combined cash flow and equity growth.

Today, David's role has shifted. Contractors and property managers run the day-to-day. His accountant oversees tax strategies and depreciation schedules. He no longer chases rent checks—he builds **legacy wealth**, structuring trusts so that his children will inherit a portfolio of properties designed to last.

What started as one experiment in a single house became a **predictable, repeatable, transformational system**.

Field Notes from David's Case

- ✅ **Systemized growth.** Defined buy box + conversion template prevented mistakes.
- ✅ **Scaled financing smartly.** HELOCs, cash flow leverage, and portfolio loans accelerated acquisitions.
- ✅ **Diversified markets.** Balanced college towns, medical hubs, resorts, and suburbs reduced risk.
- ✅ **Built strong teams.** Realtors, contractors, managers, and CPAs kept scaling efficient.
- ✅ **Shifted mindset.** Transitioned from income-focused landlord to legacy-focused wealth builder.

Bridge to Chapter 14

- **Lesson 1: Systems scale, improvisation doesn't.** Repeatability is the engine of portfolio growth.
- **Lesson 2: Leverage compounds.** Cash flow funds equity, which funds new acquisitions.
- **Lesson 3: Think beyond income.** The endgame is legacy—passing wealth, not just rent checks, to the next generation.

Why One Property Is Just the Beginning

Converting a single SFR into a multi-resident rental is powerful on its own. It can double cash flow, build equity, and provide flexible exit options. But the true wealth comes when you **repeat the process across multiple properties**. Each home becomes another stream of income, another asset on your balance sheet, and another step toward financial freedom.

Step 1: Create a Repeatable System

Every successful investor eventually discovers: systems scale, improvisation doesn't.

- **Acquisition Criteria**: Define your "buy box"—property size, price range, layout, and neighborhood characteristics.
- **Conversion Template**: Standardize your approach to design, renovations, and tenant mix.
- **Management Model**: Decide whether you'll self-manage, use property managers, or employ a hybrid system.

Investor Tip: Build checklists (like those in this book) into your acquisition and conversion process. This prevents costly mistakes and accelerates decision-making.

Step 2: Scale with Financing

- **Cash Flow Leverage**: Use the increased income from one property to qualify for financing on the next.
- **HELOCs**: Draw equity from one property to fund another conversion.
- **Partnerships**: Pool capital and share profits with trusted partners to grow faster.
- **Portfolio Loans**: Once you own several properties, some lenders offer financing based on portfolio performance rather than individual property income.

Step 3: Diversify Across Markets

Different markets offer different opportunities:

- **College Towns**: Consistent student demand.
- **Medical Hubs**: Strong appeal for traveling nurses and professionals.
- **Seasonal Resorts**: High demand during peak seasons.
- **Suburban Growth Corridors**: Families and hybrid buyers looking for flexible housing.

By diversifying, you reduce risk and ensure steady income across varying market conditions.

Step 4: Build Professional Teams

Wealth-building requires leverage—not just financial, but human.

- **Realtors**: Specialized in investment properties.
- **Contractors**: Familiar with repeatable conversions.
- **Property Managers**: Trained in by-room or multi-resident rentals.
- **Accountants/Attorneys**: Ensure tax efficiency and legal compliance.

The stronger your team, the faster and safer you scale.

Step 5: Transition from Income to Legacy

As your portfolio grows, shift your mindset:

- **From Cash Flow to Wealth**: Use income to acquire more properties, then shift toward equity growth.
- **From Active to Passive**: Outsource management, freeing your time.
- **From Investor to Legacy Builder**: Plan estate strategies, trusts, and long-term wealth transfer to future generations.

Case Study: The Conversion Portfolio

An investor began with one SFR in Riverside, California. Over 10 years:

- Converted 8 homes into multi-resident rentals.
- Averaged $2,000/month net cash flow per property.
- Held them for 5–7 years each, then sold half back as SFRs during strong markets.
- Total net gain: over $2 million in combined cash flow and equity growth.

The system, once mastered, became **predictable, scalable, and transformational**.

Investor's Checklist for Repeatability

- Defined acquisition criteria and conversion template.
- Financing strategy aligned with growth goals.
- Portfolio diversified across markets.
- Professional team assembled and leveraged.
- Long-term plan shifts from income to legacy.

Bonus Chapter: California's ADU & JADU Revolution — Turning One SFR into Many

---

1. Why This Matters for Investors

California's housing crisis has forced the state to **preempt local resistance**. Since 2017, a steady series of laws (SB 1069, AB 68, AB 881, SB 13, AB 2221, SB 9, AB 1033) have made **Accessory Dwelling Units (ADUs)** and **Junior ADUs (JADUs)** a cornerstone of housing production.

For the investor, this is not just a policy shift—it's a **structural arbitrage opportunity**. With the stroke of a permit, you can convert a single-family parcel into a **legal multi-resident income property**.

---

2. What the Law Now Permits

On a single-family lot (by right):

- **Primary dwelling** (the SFR)
- **1 JADU** (≤500 sf, carved from the main house or attached garage)
- **1 ADU (conversion)** from existing space (e.g., garage, attic, rec room)
- **1 ADU (detached)** at least 800 sf, 16–20 ft tall, 4-ft setbacks

👉 Total: **Up to 4 dwellings** on a single parcel.

Under SB 9 (duplex/lot-split law):

- Up to 2 primary units
- Local governments may allow ADUs on top, but capped at **4 units per lot**

On multifamily lots:

- Up to **8 detached ADUs** + interior "conversion ADUs" (25% of unit count)

---

3. Investor Applications

- **Urban infill:** Buy SFRs on transit-served lots → carve JADU + add detached ADU → 3–4 streams of rent.
- **Suburban plays:** Use deep lots for a detached ADU that looks like a small cottage—high rent appeal.
- **SB 9 duplex:** In neighborhoods where duplexing fits, build 2 primaries + detached ADUs for a stealth 4-plex.
- **Multifamily expansion:** If you own or acquire a small apartment, add backyard "ADU cottages" (up to 8).

---

4. Practical Investor Guidance

Design & Construction

- Always maximize **privacy + separate entrances →** easier to lease at market rents.
- Use **utility separation** (sub-metering if possible).
- Convert **attached garages** first; they're cheapest and now ministerially approved.

---

5. Legal & Compliance

- **ADU permits:** Must be approved/denied in **60 days**.
- **No impact fees** for ≤750 sf ADUs.
- **No sprinklers** if primary doesn't require them.
- **Parking exemptions** within ½-mile of transit or for conversions.
- **Rentals must be 30+ days** (no short-term).
- **HOAs cannot ban ADUs/JADUs** outright.
- **Owner-occupancy:** Required only for JADUs.

---

6. Exit & ROI

- New **AB 1033 law** lets cities opt in to allow **condo-sale of ADUs**.
- Separate mailboxes/addresses improve appraisal comps.
- ADUs **don't count toward zoning density**, helpful for resale positioning.

---

7. Key Rules That Shape Your Strategy

- **ADUs have no owner-occupancy requirement**
- **JADUs require owner occupancy + deed restriction**
- **No impact fees** for ADUs ≤750 sf
- **No sprinklers** required if the primary doesn't have them
- **Parking waived** if within ½-mile of transit or for conversions
- **60-day permit deadline** for approval/denial
- **Rentals must be 30+ days** (no STRs)
- **HOAs cannot ban ADUs** outright
- **AB 1033 (2024)**: Cities may opt in to allow **ADU condo sales**

---

8. The Investor's Advantage

- **Cash flow:** Four rent streams on one parcel, without multifamily zoning
- **Appraisal bump:** Income approach increases value at refinance or sale
- **Exit flexibility:** Condo conversion possible under AB 1033 in opt-in cities
- **Barrier reduction:** By-right permitting, fee waivers, and transit exemptions

---

Bonus Chapter A: The Investor Playbook — From Lot to Multi-Resident Cash Flow

---

1. Pre-Acquisition Checklist

- Confirm zoning: SFR with ADU rights
- Check transit map: within ½-mile = no parking required
- Verify sewer/septic capacity
- Review HOA/CC&Rs (they can't ban, but may regulate)
- Look for oversized bedrooms, garages, or deep backyards

---

2. Planning & Design

- Program the **3-unit stack** (JADU + conversion ADU + detached ADU)
- Target detached ADU ≤750 sf to avoid impact fees
- Prioritize privacy & separate entrances
- Consider sub-metering utilities

---

3. Permitting

- Submit complete plan set → starts 60-day clock
- Keep within **objective standards** (height, setbacks, design)
- Track denials: they must give curable reasons

---

4. Operations

- Market as **long-term rentals (30+ days)**
- Set up addresses, mailboxes, parking assignments
- Budget for fencing/landscaping for privacy
- Price rents by unit type (studio JADU, 1-bed conversion, 2-bed detached)

---

5. Exit Strategies

- Refinance with income-based valuation
- Sell as enhanced SFR (4-unit income property)
- If city adopted AB 1033 → condo-ize and sell ADUs individually
- Hold for appreciation, with cash flow offsetting mortgage

---

6. Deal Worksheet

Property Address: ______________________________
Lot Size: ______________________________________
Transit within ½-mile? □ Y / □ N
Garage available for conversion? □ Y / □ N
Potential JADU space? □ Y / □ N
Backyard space for 800-sf detached? □ Y / □ N
Projected unit mix: _________________________
Projected gross rents: ______________________
Projected NOI: _______________________________

---

7. Case Study

Investor A – Los Angeles Suburban Parcel

- Bought 3-bed SFR for $650k
- Added 1 JADU from existing family room (studio)
- Converted garage to 1-bed ADU
- Built 750-sf detached 2-bed ADU in back
- Now collects **$7,200/mo gross rent** across four tenants
- Property refinanced at $1.05M based on income approach

Bonus Chapter B: Sample Pro Formas for Hybrid SFR Conversions in California

---

Scenario 1: Urban Infill (Transit-Served SFR in Los Angeles)

Property: 3-bed/2-bath SFR, 1,400 sf, near Metro line
Purchase Price: $750,000

Conversion Strategy

- **JADU (studio, 450 sf)** from existing family room
- **Garage conversion ADU (1-bed, 400 sf)**
- **Detached ADU (2-bed, 800 sf)** in backyard

Estimated Costs

- JADU: $60,000 (interior reconfiguration, efficiency kitchen)
- Garage conversion: $120,000 (full conversion, plumbing tie-ins)
- Detached ADU: $220,000 (turnkey build, 800 sf @ $275/sf)
- Soft costs/permits/fees: $35,000
- **Total Investment in Additions: $435,000**

Rent Projections (market, 2025)

- JADU (studio): $1,600/mo
- Garage ADU (1-bed): $2,100/mo
- Detached ADU (2-bed): $3,000/mo
- Primary (3-bed SFR): $3,800/mo
- **Total Gross Rent: $10,500/mo ($126,000/yr)**

ROI Snapshot

- All-in basis: $1,185,000 ($750k + $435k)
- NOI (after 30% op. exp.): $88,200/yr
- **Cap Rate on Cost: 7.4%**
- Value on 5% cap: ~$1.76M
- **Equity gain on stabilization: ~$575k**

Scenario 2: Suburban SFR with Deep Lot (Riverside County)

Property: 3-bed/2-bath SFR, 1,600 sf, large 9,000 sf lot
Purchase Price: $525,000

Conversion Strategy

- **JADU (500 sf)** carved from master suite wing
- **Detached ADU (2-bed, 750 sf)** in backyard cottage style

Estimated Costs

- JADU: $70,000 (partition, kitchenette, bath)
- Detached ADU: $180,000 (750 sf @ $240/sf, no impact fees)
- Soft costs/permits: $25,000
- **Total: $275,000**

Rent Projections

- JADU (studio): $1,300/mo
- Detached ADU (2-bed): $2,100/mo
- Primary (3-bed SFR): $2,600/mo
- **Gross Rent: $6,000/mo ($72,000/yr)**

ROI Snapshot

- All-in: $800,000
- NOI (70% of gross): $50,400/yr
- **Cap Rate on Cost: 6.3%**
- Value on 5.5% cap: ~$916,000
- **Equity gain: ~$116k**, plus steady cash flow

Scenario 3: Multifamily Expansion (4-Unit in Sacramento)

Property: 4-plex (2-bed units), existing rent roll $5,800/mo
Purchase Price: $950,000

Expansion Strategy

- Add **4 detached ADUs (2-bed, 750 sf each)** at rear (deep lot)
- Use **ministerial multifamily ADU law** (up to 8 detached)

Estimated Costs

- 4 ADUs: $750,000 ($250/sf x 750 sf x 4)
- Site work/utilities: $100,000
- Soft costs/permits: $50,000
- **Total: $900,000**

Rent Projections

- Each ADU (2-bed): $2,200/mo → $8,800/mo total
- Existing 4-plex rent: $5,800/mo
- **Gross Rent: $14,600/mo ($175,200/yr)**

ROI Snapshot

- All-in: $1,850,000 ($950k + $900k)
- NOI (65% of gross): $113,880/yr
- **Cap Rate on Cost: 6.1%**
- Value on 5.25% cap: ~$2.17M
- **Equity gain: ~$320k** at stabilization, plus larger future exit

---

Bonus Chapter C: Pro Forma Case Studies

Case Study 1: Urban Infill — Los Angeles Transit-Served SFR

Property Profile

Item	Details
Property Type	3-bed / 2-bath SFR
Location	Los Angeles (near Metro)
Lot Size	Standard infill parcel
Purchase Price	$750,000

Conversion Plan & Costs

Unit	Size	Type	Est. Cost
JADU	450 sf	Studio (inside house)	$60,000
ADU (garage)	400 sf	1-bed conversion	$120,000
ADU (detached)	800 sf	2-bed new build	$220,000
Soft Costs / Permits	—	—	$35,000
Total Investment	—	—	**$435,000**

Rent Projections

Unit	Monthly Rent	Annual Rent
JADU (studio)	$1,600	$19,200
Garage ADU (1-bed)	$2,100	$25,200
Detached ADU (2-bed)	$3,000	$36,000
Primary SFR (3-bed)	$3,800	$45,600
Total Gross Rent	**$10,500**	**$126,000**

ROI Snapshot

Metric	Value
All-in Basis	$1,185,000
Net Operating Income (30% op. exp.)	$88,200
Cap Rate on Cost	7.4%
Estimated Value @ 5% Cap	$1.76M
Equity Gain on Stabilization	~$575,000

Case Study 2: Suburban Deep Lot — Riverside County SFR

Property Profile

Item	Details
Property Type	3-bed / 2-bath SFR
Location	Riverside County
Lot Size	9,000 sf (deep lot)
Purchase Price	$525,000

Conversion Plan & Costs

Unit	Size	Type	Est. Cost
JADU	500 sf	Studio (from master suite)	$70,000
ADU (detached)	750 sf	2-bed new build	$180,000
Soft Costs / Permits	—	—	$25,000
Total Investment	—	—	**$275,000**

Rent Projections

Unit	Monthly Rent	Annual Rent
JADU (studio)	$1,300	$15,600
Detached ADU (2-bed)	$2,100	$25,200
Primary SFR (3-bed)	$2,600	$31,200
Total Gross Rent	**$6,000**	**$72,000**

ROI Snapshot

Metric	Value
All-in Basis	$800,000
Net Operating Income (30% op. exp.)	$50,400
Cap Rate on Cost	6.3%
Estimated Value @ 5.5% Cap	~$916,000
Equity Gain on Stabilization	~$116,000

Case Study 3: Multifamily Expansion — Sacramento 4-Plex

Property Profile

Item	Details
Property Type	Existing 4-plex
Location	Sacramento
Purchase Price	$950,000

Expansion Plan & Costs

Unit	Size	Type	Est. Cost
4 Detached ADUs	750 sf each	2-bed cottages	$750,000
Site Work / Utilities	—	—	$100,000
Soft Costs / Permits	—	—	$50,000
Total Investment	—	—	**$900,000**

Rent Projections

Unit	Monthly Rent	Annual Rent
Existing 4-plex	$5,800	$69,600
4 Detached ADUs	$8,800	$105,600
Total Gross Rent	**$14,600**	**$175,200**

ROI Snapshot

Metric	Value
All-in Basis	$1,850,000
Net Operating Income (35% op. exp.)	$113,880
Cap Rate on Cost	6.1%
Estimated Value @ 5.25% Cap	~$2.17M
Equity Gain on Stabilization	~$320,000

Reader Worksheets

Blank Pro Forma Worksheet

Property Profile

Item	Your Numbers
Address	__________
Purchase Price	__________
Lot Size	__________
Zoning / Transit Check	__________

Conversion Plan & Costs

Unit	Size	Type	Est. Cost
JADU	___ sf	__________	$__________
ADU (conversion)	___ sf	__________	$__________
ADU (detached)	___ sf	__________	$__________
Soft Costs / Permits	—	—	$__________
Total Investment	—	—	**$__________**

Rent Projections

Unit	Monthly Rent	Annual Rent
JADU	$_____	$_____
Conversion ADU	$_____	$_____
Detached ADU	$_____	$_____
Primary Dwelling	$_____	$_____
Total Gross Rent	**$_____**	**$_____**

ROI Snapshot

Metric	Your Numbers
All-in Basis	$_________
Net Operating Income	$_________
Cap Rate on Cost	_____ %
Estimated Value @ __% Cap	$_________
Equity Gain on Stabilization	$_________

Henry Omelchenko

Conclusion - Cash Flow Today, Wealth Tomorrow: Bringing It All Together

---

When you first began reading this book, you met ordinary people—investors like Martin, Anita, David—who discovered extraordinary results by rethinking what a single-family residence could be. They stepped beyond the old "location, location, location" mantra and asked a new question: *What if one house could give me both steady rental income today and long-term equity growth tomorrow?*

That single question reshapes the way you see real estate. It reframes the humble SFR not as a static object but as a flexible **wealth-building platform**.

Over fourteen chapters you learned how to see hidden potential, design for people (not just floor plans), manage with systems, and—most importantly—protect resale value through **reversibility**.

With the **Bonus Chapters**, you now have a second engine: California's **ADU/JADU revolution**—a legal pathway to multiply income streams on a single-family parcel, often by right. Put together, these two approaches form a powerful playbook that works across market cycles.

The S2M Playbook Recap

Throughout these chapters, you've learned the **step-by-step roadmap**:

- **Assess the property** with an investor's eye (Chapters 3–4).
- **Run the numbers** to ensure feasibility and profitability (Chapter 5).
- **Design and build smartly** for multiple residents (Chapters 6–7).
- **Install systems** that minimize friction and maximize comfort (Chapter 8).
- **Attract the right tenants** and manage effectively (Chapters 9–10).
- **Optimize cash flow** while protecting resale value (Chapters 11–12).
- **Time your exits** and play the long game of equity growth (Chapter 13).
- **Scale and repeat** to transform one win into a lasting portfolio (Chapter 14).

At every turn, we've emphasized the **"secret sauce" of reversibility**—designing conversions so they can be undone, returning the property to its pure SFR form. This flexibility protects resale value, widens your buyer pool, and ensures you're never locked into one strategy.

California's ADU & JADU Revolution — A Legal Tailwind

As powerful as this playbook is on its own, something remarkable is happening—especially in California.

The **ADU (Accessory Dwelling Unit)** and **JADU (Junior ADU)** laws passed over the last decade are a once-in-a-generation policy shift. In effect, the state has written into law the very principles you've been learning in this book: **turning one single-family parcel into many income streams.**

Here's why this matters:

- On a single SFR lot, you can now **legally build or convert up to 4 dwellings**—the primary house, a JADU, a conversion ADU, and a detached ADU.
- Parking mandates have been slashed, permit timelines capped at 60 days, and impact fees waived for smaller units.
- Under **AB 1033**, cities may even allow you to **sell ADUs as condos**, unlocking exit strategies once unimaginable.
- HOAs can no longer ban ADUs outright.
- For multifamily lots, the law permits **up to 8 detached ADUs plus interior conversions**—a seismic expansion of density without rezoning battles.

In short: California has turned the "single-to-multi" concept from a creative investor strategy into a **legal entitlement.**

For you as an investor, this means:

- More opportunities on every parcel.
- Fewer regulatory roadblocks.
- Multiple paths to cash flow, refinance, resale, or even condo conversion.

The Bigger Picture — Beyond California

While California leads, other states are watching closely. Oregon, Washington, New York, and even parts of Texas have begun debating similar ADU-friendly reforms. The housing crisis isn't going away, and policy is shifting toward **density, flexibility, and affordability.** Investors who understand how to operate at the intersection of private opportunity and public policy will be positioned to win for decades to come.

The Two-Engine Playbook

Engine 1: Reversible Single-to-Multi

- **Cash flow now**: Partition oversized spaces into additional bedrooms/suites; balance baths (1:2 ratio); install smart locks, mesh Wi-Fi, and durable finishes.
- **Systems that stick**: Parking assignments, flat-fee utilities, cleaning rhythms, clear house rules, and a "house captain" if you self-manage.
- **Secret sauce**: Document everything and keep changes **non-structural**. When the market turns favorable, remove partitions, neutralize "multi" signals, and sell as an SFR to the biggest buyer pool.

Engine 2: California ADU/JADU Law (By-Right Density)

- **What's possible on an SFR lot (by right)**:
  Primary home + 1 **JADU** (≤500 sf, carved from existing space) + 1 **conversion ADU** (e.g., garage) + 1 **detached ADU** (≥800 sf, 4-ft setbacks, 16–20 ft height) → **up to 4 dwellings** on one parcel.
- **SB 9 path**: In qualifying areas, up to **2 primaries** (duplex) on a lot; some jurisdictions then allow ADUs on top (capped at 4 units per lot).
- **Multifamily lots**: Up to **8 detached ADUs** plus interior "conversion ADUs" (≈25% of existing unit count).
- **Investor-friendly guardrails**: 60-day ministerial permit decisions; no impact fees ≤750 sf; sprinkler exemptions if the primary doesn't have them; parking waived within ½-mile of transit or for conversions; HOAs can't ban

ADUs outright; rentals must be **30+ days**; JADUs require owner occupancy, ADUs do **not**.

- **AB 1033 (opt-in by city)**: Potential **condo sale** of ADUs—an exit lever that can unlock retail pricing.

Takeaway: Reversible S2M is a **design/operations strategy**; ADU/JADU is a **legal/entitlement strategy**. Use either—or both—in the same portfolio, depending on the parcel, timing, and capital.

When to Use Which (A Fast Decision Grid)

- **Tight budget / fast timeline / minimal permits?** Choose **Reversible S2M**. Light construction, quick lease-up, easy to unwind for resale.
- **Deep lot / garage / near transit / patient capital?** Pursue **ADU stack** (JADU + conversion ADU + detached ADU). Higher capex, but durable value, clearer appraisals, and potential condo exits (AB 1033, where adopted).
- **Soft market (buyers cautious, inventory high)?** **Hold** and cash flow—by-room or ADU rents stabilize returns.
- **Hot market (low inventory, family demand strong)?** **Reverse** S2M signals, market as SFR (or sell ADUs if local AB 1033 path exists), and capture top-end pricing.

Appraisal & Exit Strategy, Upgraded

- **SFR comps** typically price higher than income-only investor comps. That's why reversibility matters.
- **Income approach** shines when you've added legal ADUs/JADUs—steady, documented rent streams support refinance or sale.
- **AB 1033** (if your city opts in) can **unlock retail condo pricing** for ADUs, creating staggered exits and liquidity without selling the primary.

The Risk Controls That Protect Your Upside

- **Compliance first**: Zoning, occupancy caps, egress, detectors, permits. (Penalties and disclosure issues kill deals.)
- **Reversible design**: Non-load-bearing partitions, no full kitchens in bedrooms, curb appeal that reads as SFR.
- **Cost discipline**: Durable mid-grade materials; scope control; documented warranties.
- **Systems**: Parking maps, flat-fee utilities, smart tech, scheduled cleaning, house rules, and a "house captain" or PM.
- **Documentation**: A Conversion/ADU binder with plans, permits, photos, receipts—gold for appraisers and buyers.

Putting It All Together: A 90-Day Action Plan

Days 1–30 — Pipeline & Feasibility

1. Define your **buy box** (layout, utility capacity, garage, lot depth, proximity to transit/employers).
2. Underwrite two cases per target: **Reversible S2M** *and* **ADU stack**.
3. Speak with planning: confirm **ADU/JADU standards**, SB 9 eligibility, and any objective design rules.
4. Get contractor + electrician to do a **systems stress test** (panel, HVAC, plumbing).

Days 31–60 — Design & Approval

1. Choose the path: quick **S2M** (6–10 weeks) or **ADU** (ministerial, usually 60-day clock).
2. Lock your **tenant niche** (nurses, grad students, professionals) and pre-market rooms/units.
3. Build your **Reversal File** or **ADU Plan Set** from day one.

Days 61–90 — Execution & Systems

1. Install privacy + soundproofing; balance **bathrooms** to ~1:2 ratio.
2. Set **parking**, **utility fee**, **smart locks**, **mesh Wi-Fi**, and **house rules** before move-ins.
3. Snapshot **before/after** photos and keep all receipts for taxes and future exit.

California ADU/JADU Quick Reference (An Investor Lens)

- **By right** on SFR lots: Primary + **JADU** (≤500 sf) + **conversion ADU** + **detached ADU (≥800 sf)** → up to **4 dwellings**.
- **60-day** permit decision; **no impact fees ≤750 sf**; **no sprinklers** if the primary doesn't have them.
- **Parking waived** within ½-mile of transit or for conversions.
- **30+ day** minimum rental terms (no STRs).
- **JADU** requires owner occupancy; **ADUs do not**.
- **AB 1033** (city opt-in): possible **condo sale** of ADUs—plan utility separation and addresses if you want this option later.

The Philosophy That Wins in Any Market

1. **Engineer ROI**: Don't hope for it. Design for privacy, flow, and comfort to command premium rents.
2. **Protect the Exit**: Every modification should be easy to unwind—or fully permitted to support valuation.
3. **Leverage Law**: Where ADU/JADU rules apply, legal density is value. Use it.
4. **Document Everything**: Great records lower risk, improve appraisals, and convince buyers.
5. **Scale with Systems**: Repeatability—not improvisation—creates exponential wealth.

Closing Story — *Your Chapter Begins Now*

Imagine this: You're standing in the driveway of an ordinary SFR. To most buyers, it's just a house. To you, it's a **multi-resident opportunity**, a **cash-flow engine**, and one day, a **resalable family home**.

You can almost see the blueprint overlay:

- A quiet JADU carved from the main house.
- A detached ADU tucked neatly into the backyard.
- A garage conversion that works now, but can be restored later.
- Tenants bringing steady income today.
- A future buyer—whether a family or an investor—ready to pay top dollar tomorrow.

That's the essence of this strategy. That's *Cash Flow Today, Wealth Tomorrow*.

The tools, stories, laws, and systems are now in your hands. The next chapter isn't mine to write—it's yours.

📝 Action Plan: Cash Flow Today, Wealth Tomorrow

The Investor's Quick-Hit Checklist

---

1. Pre-Acquisition

☑ Define your **buy box**: size, layout, neighborhood, price.
☑ Confirm **zoning** and check for ADU/JADU rights.
☑ Review **HOA/CC&Rs** for restrictions.
☑ Inspect for **structural adaptability**: oversized bedrooms, garages, basements, deep lots.

---

2. Financial Feasibility

☑ Run **Gross Potential Rent (GPR)** projections (SFR vs. multi-resident).
☑ Estimate **conversion costs** + add a 10–15% contingency.
☑ Calculate **ROI and payback period**.
☑ Line up **financing** (cash, HELOC, portfolio loan, partnerships).

---

3. Legal & Compliance

☑ Verify **occupancy limits** and rental regulations.
☑ Pull **permits** for construction or ADU conversions.
☑ Ensure **safety compliance**: egress, detectors, fire codes.
☑ Use California ADU/JADU fast-track rules (60-day approvals, no parking near transit).

---

4. Design & Build

☑ Prioritize **privacy** (soundproofing, locks, entrances).
☑ Balance **common areas** (kitchen, laundry, lounge).
☑ Achieve bathroom ratio: **1 bath per 2 tenants**.
☑ Furnish strategically (by-room = furnished, long-term = unfurnished).
☑ Document everything in a **conversion binder**.

---

5. Systems & Management

☑ Plan **parking & access** assignments.
☑ Decide on **utility billing** (bundled, flat fee, or sub-meter).
☑ Install **smart tech**: locks, thermostats, Wi-Fi mesh.
☑ Write **house rules** + establish conflict resolution.
☑ Choose your management model: self, professional, or hybrid.

---

6. Optimization

☑ Add **rent premiums** for furnished rooms or en-suites.
☑ Create **add-on revenue**: parking, laundry, cleaning services.
☑ Reduce expenses: efficiency upgrades, preventive maintenance.
☑ Review tax strategy with a **real estate CPA**.

---

7. Exit Strategy

☑ Maintain reversibility with non-load-bearing walls + capped plumbing.
☑ Budget for **restoration costs** before resale.
☑ Stage and market as **SFR + optional income property**.
☑ Time the market: hold in buyer's market, sell in seller's market.
☑ Explore **ADU condo conversion** if local laws allow (AB 1033).

✅ **Remember:** One house can be two strategies in one—cash flow now, wealth later. Start small, systemize, and scale. Your path to *Cash Flow Today, Wealth Tomorrow* begins with the next property you evaluate.

About the Author:

"Henry Omelchenko has helped local homeowners unlock hidden cash flow and long-term equity through his Single-to-Multi Conversion Strategy for two decades. His practical real estate strategies have shown our clients how to build financial freedom from the houses they already own." – **The Elder Law Group**

Henry Omelchenko

Henry Omelchenko started his real estate journey like many others — buying single-family homes with hopes of steady appreciation. Along the way, he discovered a smarter path: converting ordinary houses into flexible, multi-resident properties that generate income today while protecting value for tomorrow. With a background in both investing and property management, Henry shares practical, real-world strategies anyone can use, whether you're buying your first home or scaling your portfolio. His mission is simple: to show homeowners and investors how to create wealth from properties they already own — or ones they're about to buy.

Made in the USA
Monee, IL
04 November 2026

67387181R00079